Praise for *Seeing Sense: Visual literacy as a tool for libraries, learning and reader development*

'*Seeing Sense* is an invaluable addition to any librarian or teacher's CPD library. Not only does it enhance understanding of this neglected topic, but the clarity and lucidity of the exposition make this an enjoyable and fascinating read. Both philosophical and highly practical, this is a very rich resource, supplemented by witness statements from artists and illustrators and relevant case studies which show how applying the tenets of visual literacy to library and classroom practice can reap rewards and engage readers. The reader is given a thorough grounding in the technical language of the visual arts, and the deeper awareness of all the processes involved will make it essential reading for future CILIP Kate Greenaway Medal judges and all those who nominate for the awards.'
Joy Court, Editor of Reading by Reading *and* Read to Succeed, *Reviews Editor of* The School Librarian, *UKLA Trustee*

'"No visual literacy, no democracy. It's a simple as that." So writes Philip Pullman in the foreword to this marvellously clear and full account of the role of visual literacy in culture. In our increasingly visual world, we all need to be able to decode images to understand their effects. Jake Hope uses interviews and case studies of those who make, publish and mediate picture books, to show how the very first art form children encounter can be harnessed to help them learn and acquire the skills they need to navigate the world. From Lancashire to Singapore environments and innovations in how to bring children and books together at home, in educational settings, in libraries and in digitally created environments are described and practical advice provided. This book truly is replete with information and insights.'
Professor Kim Reynolds, Professor of Children's Literature, Newcastle University, Past President of International Research Society for Children's Literature

'The power of illustration should never be underestimated. When you gaze into the eyes of a character on a page, you make a deeper connection which builds empathy and understanding. *Seeing Sense* is an engaging and compelling read for anyone who wants to explore how pictures add rich depth and nuance to narrative and indeed, tell their own story. It will be a hugely valuable resource for librarians, teachers and all those passionate about inspiring young readers.'
Sarah Mears, Programme Manager at Libraries Connected, co-founder of Empathy Lab

D1423975

'*Seeing Sense* is essential reading for all librarians working with children and young people, other educators and anybody with an interest in visual literacy. Showing that visual literacy is a tool that is used by everybody on a daily basis and is an essential component to the process of "growing" readers, Hope provides an insight into the many facets of the term in an accessible and illuminating manner.

With contributions from a host of respected illustrators, authors, publishers, graphic designers and other experts, rich and fascinating insights into the creative process are offered. This is a comprehensive guide to visual literacy, looking at a broad range of factors, including in-depth and fascinating explorations of the evolution of picture books, from concept to marketing; current theories and approaches to developing reading ability AND a love of reading; using visuals to create engaging environments for young people, and an extensive glossary.

Showing the importance and power of visual literacy and how it enriches and enhances throughout our lives, *Seeing Sense* is a strong rebuttal to any suggestion that pictures are merely a stepping stone to, or decoration of, the written word. Perfect for any librarian who has ever had to argue what constitutes a "proper" book!'
Amy McKay, CILIP Carnegie and Kate Greenaway co-ordinator, School Library Association Board Member, School Librarian of the Year 2016

'*Seeing Sense* is a comprehensive and fascinating study of the importance of visual literacy and the power contained in illustrated texts to enrich the reading experience and broaden both perceptions and understanding. It will be equally useful to librarians, teachers and illustration students; many of today's most talented artists and illustrators have lent their own insights to what is a seminal text on the subject. Having the confidence and discernment to *see* and *feel* the multi-layering and integrity of illustration, and to appreciate that there is more to this than the picture books associated with under 5s' primary reading experience (though these are extremely valuable in themselves), is at the heart of what is also an immersive read and an essential handbook which covers a range of material. From the human eye and aspects of colour, to board and tactile books, to the role of illustration in promoting diversity and representation, *Seeing Sense* has relevance beyond a UK readership and will be invaluable to any professional delivering visual literacy training.'
Alison Brumwell, Chair of Youth Libraries Group, contributor to Reading by Right

Seeing Sense

Seeing Sense

Visual literacy as a tool for libraries, learning and reader development

Jake Hope

facet
publishing

© Jake Hope 2020

Published by Facet Publishing, 7 Ridgmount Street, London WC1E 7AE
www.facetpublishing.co.uk

Facet Publishing is wholly owned by CILIP: the Library and Information Association.

British Library Cataloguing in Publication Data
A catalogue record for this book is available from the British Library.

ISBN 978-1-78330-441-7 (paperback)
ISBN 978-1-78330-442-4 (hardback)
ISBN 978-1-78330-443-1 (e-book)

First published 2020

Text printed on FSC accredited material.

The cover of the book has been generously created by Olivia Lomenech Gill and features famous illustrations from the world of children's books reimagined as much loved toys. These include the Paddington Bear soft toy © Paddington and Company Limited; 'The Tiger Who Came to Tea' created by Judith Kerr and published by HarperCollins Children's Books; and The Snowman created by Raymond Briggs and published by Puffin Children's Books.

Typeset from author's files in 11/14pt Revival 565 and Frutiger by Flagholme Publishing Services.
Printed and made in Great Britain by CPI Group (UK) Ltd, Croydon, CR0 4YY.

Dedicated to Jackie Morris

Contents

List of figures, boxes and case studies

Figures

Boxes

Case studies

Acknowledgements

Those who have helped with quotes, research and insight into their working practices are numerous, many thanks.

Jon Agee

Laurence Anholt

Steve Antony

Peter Bently

Stephen Biesty

Freya Blackwood

Quentin Blake

Benedict Blathwayt

BookTrust

Ruth Brown

Anthony Browne

Alison Brumwell

Centre for Literacy in Primary Education

Lauren Child

Frank Cottrell-Boyce

Joy Court

Cressida Cowell

Alice Curry

Nicola Davies

Eva Eland

David Fickling

Anne Fine

Klaus Flugge

Debbie Foy

Vivian French

Adele Geras

Mel Gibson

Debi Gliori

Prue Goodwin

Antonia Gray

Charlotte Hacking

Ziggy Hanaor

Mererid Hopwood

Petr Horacek

Shirley Hughes

Oliver Jeffers

Steve Jenkins

Natalie Jones

Sarah Lawrance

Olivia Lomenech Gill

Jessica Love

Ali Mawle

Sarah McIntyre

Amy McKay

Robert MacFarlane

Poonam Mistry

Jackie Morris

Chris Mould

Adam Murphy

Ifeoma Onyefulu

Sarah Packenham

Greet Pawelijn

Isobel Powell

Philip Pullman
Ben Reed
Gillian Rennie
Chris Riddell
Anna Ridley
Philip Ridley
David Roberts
Edward Ross
Seven Stories
Nick Sharratt
Cate Simmonds
Art Spiegelman
Mike Stirling

Alex Strick
Morag Styles
Bryan Talbot
Zoe Tucker
Nick Ward
David Wiesner
Wild in Art
Vicki Willden-Lebrecht
Jessica Woollard
Gene Luen Yang
Yu Rong
Yuval Zommer

Foreword

Philip Pullman

Only the other day I came across the expression 'physical literacy'. Apparently it means being able to run and jump and catch and so on, and the phrase has been in use for five years at least. I remember when the word 'oracy' came in – it must have been in the 80s – and we all had to learn what it meant and make sure it was attended to. No doubt there are more –acies on their way, and we shall have to deal with them when they turn up. I suppose the suffix means 'the capacity, opportunity, or vocabulary to talk about something we all used to do without thinking about it'.

Some of these terms will be more useful than others. But visual literacy is an idea that both makes sense and is interesting to talk about. How do we read a picture? How do we read the graphic symbols that we see in every advertisement, on every screen, in every comic? Unlike words and sentences, these things don't have to be taught and learned (or tested – yet): they don't seem to need any pedagogy at all.

Take a little visual convention like the difference between the speech balloon and the thought bubble. Did we have to be taught what they meant? As far as I can remember, I worked it out for myself, and thought at once how clever I was. Somewhat later I thought how clever the person who invented it was. One of the ancestors of the speech balloon was the long scroll emerging from the mouth of Thomas Cranmer being burned at the stake in the illustrations to *Foxe's Book of Martyrs* (1563), but no doubt there were others. It works because it's so easy to understand.

Or take a short wavy line. What does that mean? It's not like a word, whose meaning we can look up in a dictionary. But in the context of one frame of a comic it could depict a single hair on a bald head, in another the sound of a bird singing, in yet another the powerful aroma of a gorgonzola cheese, in one yet further the disturbance of the air caused by someone running very fast. We don't need to have any of them explained, because the device is so expressive and so effortless to read, and so independent of language too: they are one of the aspects of comics that don't need translation.

Some aspects of visual literacy, then, seemed to spring into existence as they were needed, and their purpose was always to clarify storytelling. Comics are one of the best media ever in which to tell stories. I'm amazed at how long it took the comics form to arrive, considering that stories had been printed on paper for over four hundred years, and so had pictures.

But they do have their limitations. Pictures have only a present tense: they can show an action taking place, but they can't easily show whether it happens often, or seldom, or happens once and then never again, unless there are some words around, possibly in a frame caption. Pictures are good at showing space and words are good at showing time; the most sophisticated comics (such as Art Spiegelman's *Maus*) have learned how to layer all their elements in a form of counterpoint that deals with both time and space, and in which nothing is redundant and everything is expressive.

We live at a time when there are more pictures about than ever before in human history. The same is true of music, of course. When we needed the presence of a live human being who could play an instrument before we could listen to music, and when pictures depended on there being someone around who could draw, those things were rarer and perhaps more highly valued. The existence of the smart phone, which can both play you any kind of music you desire and let you make pictures both still and moving of whatever's happening in front of you, has changed everything.

But we need to understand what pictures do, and how devices like the short wavy line work, or else we'll be at the mercy of those who want us to vote for them, or sell us things, or who have motives more sinister. If it had been as easy in Greek and Roman times to make and share pictures as it is now, visual literacy would have been taught and studied as an important part of rhetoric – an essential aid to understanding and functioning well in the social and political world. Those who scoffingly dismiss 'media studies' as unworthy of academic attention either don't know their history, or don't want us to know it. No visual literacy, no democracy: it's as simple as that.

Figure 0.1 *'Illustrations illuminate books', an original illustration and quote by Chris Riddell*

CHAPTER 1

In the Frame: what is visual literacy and why does it matter?

Picture stories echo the way the brain works. We think in a combination of words and pictures and comics are a gateway drug to literacy.

(Art Spiegelman, 2019)

It is easy to take for granted how attuned we are to recognising and decoding visual stimuli, so embedded is this routine in our daily practices. The acquisition of literacy can mean that the role of images becomes devalued or dismissed, seen as something which serves purely to decorate, or embellish writing. Worse still, images can be seen as a means for cheating or bypassing comprehension of written language. As the ability to decode writing grows, the focus and educational or cultural value placed upon pictures often diminishes. Equally, however, the synergy that operates between written and pictorial language can convey complex meaning, requiring simultaneous consideration that can feel overwhelming and difficult to articulate.

Visuals can enrich and enhance the imaginative and informative worlds of reading. This provides rich opportunities not just for consumption, but for immersion and creativity too. They can provide aids for comprehension and for the retention and memorisation of information. This book explores the potency and power of visual literacy and ways this can be harnessed to create inclusive opportunities for reading and writing, building immersive worlds of knowledge and imagination and equipping practitioners and interested parties with a language to better express the creative decisions both in making, and reading, visual texts.

An introduction to *Seeing Sense*

Exploration and understanding of visual literacy is a burgeoning field that is seeing exciting development in the area of children's books, education and librarianship. It holds great potential for making reading available and accessible to a wide range of people. There is however, a distinct lack of published texts on this subject to bring together the discourse around visual literacy and provide the terminology needed to unify and further this discussion. This book draws on my personal experience working as the Reading and Learning Development Manager for Lancashire Libraries and my involvement with the CILIP Carnegie and Kate Greenaway Medals.

While working for Lancashire County Council, I organised a yearlong promotion with visual literacy as the focus. This involved exhibitions centred on visual imagery, the creation of new visual assets within the libraries and different approaches taken to enhance displays and events through visual means. When launching this yearlong promotion, training the staff felt an important starting point and it became clear through doing this that there was a sense of uncertainty around the term 'visual literacy' and the contributions it could make as part of our offer to readers. Noticing this need for a training resource and guide to visual literacy for librarians and practitioners, I set about writing this book and my hope is that it will help to build and grow an understanding and confidence in this area.

Visual literacy is a broad topic spanning numerous areas of practice so in order to capture some of the dynamism of the subject, I felt it was important to solicit the expertise of external experts in the field and, in particular, creators, who could provide insights into their practices and influences. Numerous creators have provided input into this book. This has a dual purpose, firstly in providing readers with richness of insight into their techniques and views, but secondly equipping readers with a bank of key figures that have contributed to the field of visual literacy, its growth and development. The contributors provide a rich base to explore a range of styles and approaches.

I conducted personal interviews with a number of creators and external experts and collected case studies to showcase areas of good practice within the field of visual literacy; these case studies take place in the library and other related settings. This combination of personal accounts and case studies helps to build a rich basis for furthering the dialogue around visual literacy as well as providing inspiration and practical tips for librarians and practitioners to incorporate into their provision.

The book draws on examples of visual literacy as part of our daily life and the way that we understand and interpret the world; it considers how visual literacy is used in a learning context, as a feature for design and in visual narratives – including comics, graphic novels and picturebooks. When referring to picturebooks throughout this book, I express the term as one word, a practice adopted by a number of researchers in the field. 'Picturebooks' denotes a type of book that encompasses the idea of text, illustration and design coming together holistically to provide a single creative unit.

The book begins in Chapter 1 by taking readers on a journey to understand more about the background of visual literacy and images as a means for communication. This introductory chapter outlines the various types of visual literacy and plots the origins of visual literacy from primitive cave paintings through to its role in the digital age and its impact on society. Chapter 2 explores terminology and its use in helping us to better comprehend and articulate some of the mechanics of illustrated narratives. In Chapter 3, I explore the ways in which children develop as readers from a pre-reader to expert and how visual literacy can provide a framework for developing competencies alongside this. Chapter 4 explores the influences and insights of people and processes that shape visual narratives and includes an in-depth look at how *The Lost Words* by Robert MacFarlane and Jackie Morris was created and published. As globalisation yields greater influence on the movement and experiences of individuals, Chapter 5 considers the importance of visual representation and inclusion.

In Chapter 6, I reflect on the role of Book Awards and Prizes as a means for helping to raise the profile and visibility of titles and explore some of the key global illustration awards. Chapter 7 looks at the role of visual literacy as a means for learning and conveying information and how this can be applied in a library setting. Finally, the book concludes in Chapter 8 with a look at how to create library spaces or reading spaces, which capitalise on visual literacy, drawing upon a range of case studies. It is my hope that a greater understanding of visual literacy will help readers to see the world of books, reading and their promotion from a perspective that can be inclusive, imaginative and inspiring.

Origins of visual literacy

The origins of the term visual literacy are credited to John Debes, founder of the International Visual Literacy Association. Debes (1969) defined visual literacy as follows:

> Visual Literacy refers to a group of vision-competencies a human being can develop by seeing and at the same time having and integrating other sensory experiences. The development of these competencies is fundamental to normal human learning. When developed, they enable a visually literate person to discriminate and interpret the visible actions, objects, symbols, natural or man-made, that he encounters in his environment. Through the creative use of these competencies, he is able to communicate with others. Through the appreciative use of these competencies, he is able to comprehend and enjoy the masterworks of visual communication.

Despite the relative newness of the term itself, the concept ties back to the origins of recorded human communication with primitive art and cave paintings. Visual literacy is inextricably linked with what is generally considered the origins of children's literature – illustrated instructional books, bestiaries and histories.

Alongside visual literacy's long-history, recognition of the role and appeal of illustrated work for children can be traced through various examples of historic literature. The eponymous Jane in Charlotte Bronte's *Jane Eyre* (1847) possesses herself 'of a volume, taking care that it should be one stored with pictures.' Famously, Lewis Carroll's Alice in *Alice's Adventures in Wonderland* (1865) questions 'what is the use of a book… without pictures or conversations?' Likewise, Colin in *The Secret Garden* (1911) 'was always reading and looking at pictures in splendid books.' Concepts underpinning visual literacy and an awareness of its appeal and importance as a facet of reading have long existed.

Visual literacy in the digital age

In the digital age where stories, knowledge and culture intersect and cross different platforms and art forms, visual literacy can act as a catalyst to excite and stimulate great interest and broad appeal. The opening ceremony of the London 2012 Olympics, directed by Danny Boyle, displayed this powerfully when figures from children's literature – from Harry Potter, Peter Pan and Mary Poppins to Chitty Chitty Bang Bang – were brought to life as part of a carnival-like parade, an exuberant dance spectacle that blazed onto the world stage. This visual spectacle conveyed the cultural and social value of images. In conversations with screenwriter and Carnegie medal winning novelist, Frank Cottrell-Boyce (2019), who wrote the script for the opening ceremony, he described how Danny

Boyle wanted to include a section of the ceremony that focused on the National Health Service and that this needed to be emotional given that the service embraces births and deaths. This led to discussions around bedtime stories, dreams and being read to. Frank explained:

> We wanted visual images that were strong enough to evoke a whole story, almost as though they were dehydrated. All those which we chose had such strong visuals that they became shorthand for the stories – a Victorian lady with an umbrella instantly becomes Mary Poppins. Strong visual identity makes it easier to dress up and bring characters out of the books and into play.

Likewise, in 2019, the BBC Proms featured a multi-art form concert built around Robert Macfarlane and Jackie Morris's book, *The Lost Words*, showing how both visual and verbal language can bridge different forms, creating an immersive and beguiling extravaganza for audiences of all ages. Visual literacy can enhance existing written and recorded forms of communication making it memorable and ensuring it is capable of conveying complex and data rich information about the human experience and society. As well as enhancing and working alongside written and verbal communication, visual imagery is a powerful form for conveying messages in and of its own right. An ability to encounter and decipher multi literacies is a key part of leading a rich life in modern society.

Discussing the power and appeal of words and pictures, author and illustrator, Laurence Anholt (2019), talked about his fascination with the relationship that exists between the two:

> Words and pictures have always been my twin passions – in my mind, they are inseparable. I spent eight years at art school, culminating in a Master's Degree from the Royal Academy, and always, I have been a reader. When my own children were born back in the 1980s I was drawn to picture books – where else do words and pictures co-exist so beautifully? In a good picture book, the text and illustrations run side by side, almost like a footpath following a stream. I like to think of young readers taking a magical journey alongside that winding path.

Becoming visually literate

In our everyday lives we are surrounded by visual signs, symbols and stimuli. Some of this seems almost hard-wired into us, as if pre-programmed. For example, creatures with aposematic colouring or markings are natures warning of toxicity; the fact that we read red as danger; that spiders and snakes instil fear amidst many. We build upon these rudiments as we make sense of the world, acquiring understanding that allows us to infer appropriate action. For instance, at a pedestrian crossing the red standing figure indicates possible danger and we understand as pedestrians that we should wait as it is not safe to cross, while the illumination of the green walking figure tells us it is now safe to continue our journey and cross the road.

Some symbols are more abstract and require an understanding of societal conventions: take a look inside the garments of clothing you are wearing, for instance, and you will invariably see a label with symbols. This may include a cross section of a tub with a wavy line indicating washing instructions, a triangle denoting bleach instructions, a square with a circle inside indicating drying instructions, a representation of an iron to indicate ironing instructions and a circle for dry cleaning instructions. We build a convention of understanding around these symbols, making it possible for clothing manufacturers to utilise them to convey a complex series of information and instructions within a small space. These pictorial graphics transcend the barriers of written or verbal language and so can convey messaging internationally across vast geographies and cultures. Navigating visual messaging such as this is necessary as part of our day to day existence, as Lynell Burmark suggests:

> It's no longer enough to read and write text. Our students must learn to process both words *and* pictures. To be visually literature, they must learn to 'read' (consume/interpret) images and 'write' (produce/use) visually rich communications. They must be able to move gracefully and fluently between text and images, between literal and figurative worlds.
>
> (Burmark, 5, 2008)

We are immersed in a visual, often highly designed society, from the magazines we read, the packaging that entices us, to the food we eat and the entertainment we enjoy – whether television, films, computer games or apps. Our waking and sleeping lives are built around images carrying messages to instruct, persuade, tell a story or to paint a picture of a place, time, person or lifestyle.

In conversation with academic, Morag Styles, we discussed how picture-books build an immersive interplay between images and text. Morag recalled Barbara Bader's (1976) definition of picturebooks (below) which is most commonly referred to in research literature with a focus on young readers, and the definition that, Morag states, she subscribes to most heartily:

> A picturebook is text, illustrations, total design; an item of manufacture and a commercial product; a social, cultural, historical document; and foremost an experience for a child. As an art form it hinges on the interdependence of pictures and words, on the simultaneous display of two facing pages, and on the drama of the turning page.

Bader's definition reminds us of the complexities involved with crafting picturebooks and visual stimuli. Essential to this immersive experience is the interaction with, and interpretations by, the visual reader. As readers, we become so adept at decoding visual information that it is easy to see patterns that might not even have been intended. How often in childhood have people idled time gazing up at the sky and imagining clouds to be shapes or objects? Indeed, the psychological Rorschach test, commonly known as the ink-blot test, seeks to determine personality traits through accumulating what individuals perceive across numerous abstract images. We are increasingly using visual icons to infer emotions; using a simple colon : and bracket) we recognise aspects of human facial expressions and emotion and we are able to attribute different feelings depending upon its construction, :) or :(.

Our world is coloured and shaped by the types of images that we see. This informs our architecture, fashion and art and has both potency and commercial value through its global application regardless of the language that individuals speak or read. Kate Greenaway award winning illustrator, Jackie Morris (2019), discusses the ability of images and visual symbols to transcend the cultural specificity of spoken and written language:

> While words often need translation, and are often interpreted in many varieties of ways (reading between the lines) images need no translation, they speak across land borders and language borders, and across time. We may struggle to interpret the written languages of those who have lived before us, while the images painted on to the walls of caves still resonate deep in our souls. Images cross borders in ways that words struggle to.

It could be argued that this timeless quality of images brings us back to the fundaments of language itself, with Saussure's theory of linguistics that a signifier – the word as meaning – and the signified – the object it refers to – become bound in an act of union in a process called signification. The visual is an important facet in this process as part of the apparatus that shapes our understanding of the world. Visual literacy engages us actively in semiotics, the study of signs and symbols and the meanings these convey. In his theory of individual learning styles, Walter Burke Barbe identifies visuals as one of three learning modalities: visualising, auditory and kinaesthetic (Barbe et al., 1979). Visual learners use images and visuals to better understand meaning whether these be pictures, shapes, sculptures, colours or charts. It is true for all, however, that reading is inherently a visual experience.

The origins of our relationship with visual information extends through history and pre-history. The next part of this chapter considers the history of visual literacy and its role in society, followed by an exploration of the types of visual literacy and how they are used.

From cave to computer screen: a potted guide to visual literacy in society

In Rudyard Kipling's 'How the Alphabet was Made', from his collection of *Just So Stories* (1902), Neolithic man Tegumai Bopsulai states: 'if this game of ours is going to be what I think it will, the easier we make our sound-pictures the better for everybody.'

Sound pictures are an apt way to describe some of the early recordings that happened with images. Visual literacy pre-dates writing; the oldest known, surviving example of a figurative picture is on a limestone cave in Lubang Jeriji Saléh in Borneo and depicts a bull. It is believed to be over 40,000 years old. Similar paintings portraying animals have been found in Chauvet-Pont-d'arc Cave in the Ardèche of France and the Gilf Kebir in Libya. Ochre and pigments were used as the medium to create the images. It is not clear exactly what these images were recording – whether they illustrated hunts that had happened, (this seems unlikely as remains found suggested animals most regularly encountered by the prehistoric people at such sites were often different to those depicted) or whether it was a form of wish fulfilment for a good hunt. Visual images were evidently an important method for recording experience and showing systems of belief.

This can also be seen in the discovery of prehistoric sculptures of the Venus of Willendorf, the name given to a female figurine that was found by archaeologist, Joseph Szombathy in 1908. The statue was carved from oolitic limestone and given colour through tints of ochre. The emphasis placed upon body organs relating to fertility led to the interpretation that its origins and purpose were linked to fertility rites. Similar iconography relating to fertility has been discovered on paintings and ornate designs on pottery. Archaeologists have discerned that it is likely this figure held social, political and religious significance.

Determining definitive meaning from art, however, can be difficult, as seen in the examples from antiquity above; indeed, art is arguably reliant upon a multiplicity of references and possible interpretations. The development of ideograms – graphical symbols that represent an idea – allowed more specific meaning and messages to be conveyed in a less figurative way and in a form that was more stylised yet simplified. Proto-writing, an early form of recording based around visual symbols and dating back to the Early Bronze age, used simple images to record spoken ideas. Cuneiform script was one method of using such images. These were often recorded in a medium like soft clay using basic apparatus, such as sticks, as an early stylus.

Ancient Egyptian hieroglyphs are perhaps the most well-known example of pictograms. Their meaning was lost to history for a long time. Hieroglyphs contain logographic elements; these were characters that represented a word or phrase. Some forms of written language continue to use these elements such as Chinese Hanzi. Hypothesis has been made that Egyptian hieroglyphs grew out of the culture's artistic tradition with parallels existing between these and the artistic symbols depicted on examples of pottery from the Gerzeh culture of the Sahara, which was notable for the decorative elements adorning its pottery. As well as being carved into masonry, hieroglyphs were produced on wood and papyrus and used to convey religious messages.

The Rosetta stone, discovered in 1799 in el-Rashid on the Mediterranean coast in Egypt, was one of the keys to unlocking the code of Ancient Egyptian hieroglyphs. The stone has a passage celebrating an Egyptian pharaoh and listing the great and philanthropic deeds the pharaoh had overseen for priests and people of Egypt. The script is recorded in three translations: two in Egyptian scripts, hieroglyphics and demotic, and another in Ancient Greek. In many ways the Rosetta stone shows us a turning point between ideographic (pictorial), and alphabetic (letter-based), language.

As more formal alphabets and writings began to develop this meant there were those who could and those who could not read and write: the literate and the illiterate. Reading was often associated with people in positions of power or of stature. Illustrations still had a valuable role to play in helping to convey messages to the masses and were sometimes used in ornate ways to help to show the prestige and value of the written words. This can be seen clearly in examples like *The Book of Kells* or the *Lindisfarne Gospels* both notable for their lavish production. *The Book of Kells* has a highly illuminated style, and is known for its use of full-page miniatures and the rich, varied use of colour palette drawing upon varying hues of purple, reds, greens and yellows. *The Lindisfarne Gospels* is produced on vellum with colours produced from both mineral and vegetable extracts including gold, which is used to illuminate small details. In addition to carrying written religious tracts, the books have an opulence that can clearly be discerned and is immediately apparent without needing to read the text itself.

Development of technology with wood cuts and the early printing presses meant that the written word became more common and brought production costs down as reproductions were able to be mechanised, involving significantly less manual labour and production. With the printed word now capable of being mass-produced, literacy was becoming accessible to more individuals.

As the division between readers and non-readers was so strongly aligned with divisions between those with wealth and status and the lowly, it helps to explain some of the stigma that is often attached to visual imagery. Forms which convey meaning primarily through graphic and visual means, as opposed to written, are often seen as having less significance or worth. There is sometimes a perception that picturebooks and illustrations are only tools on the journey to acquiring standard literacy, arguably part of a cultural inheritance associated with the reach of those for whom literacy was attainable. This is something Frank Serafini (2015), makes a strong argument against:

> Literacy educators need to develop children's repertoire of reading strategies beyond the decoding of written language to address the visual images and graphic design features found in contemporary picturebooks if they are to become successful readers.

With the development of information and communication technology, opportunities for creating and subsequently reading multimodal texts have abounded. Millions of gradations of colour upon screens, images can now be reproduced to look real or even hyper-real. As visual icons and images are being used as the navigation base for almost every digital device, the continued importance of imagery in contemporary times and in the future, seems secure.

The weighting of a language predicated on visual imagery feels to have a heightened significance. When SMS (short message service) became a common communication technology, each individual message was capped at a length of 160 characters, although multiple messages could be sent together. This necessitated short and simplified texts to convey meaning. Emoticons, pictorial representations, often of facial expressions, using punctuation marks like colons and brackets, were a popular and common way to convey emotion and tone in a succinct way. As technology has developed and there is a greater capacity to transfer more data, these have developed into more pictorially sophisticated emojis (also known as smileys). These 'emoticons' have become a useful tool in carrying out quick evaluation of services or activities for children. Using symbols to represent different facial expressions and tick boxes, young people can quickly and easily convey their thoughts and feelings. This visual shorthand offers an experience that has a universality that offers great potential for those working to promote reading. It can act as an equaliser, allowing readers of varying ages and abilities to access the dynamic forms and formats through which meaning is conveyed.

From pre-historic cave markings to digitised emojis, visual literacy has universal significance as a communication tool and in helping people to decode and understand the world around them. It looks certain that visual literacy will continue to play a key role in communication in the future.

Types of visual literacy
Broadly speaking visual literacy can be split into three distinct categories: functional, aesthetic and narratological. These are explored in more detail below.

Functional visual literacy
Functional visual literacy tries to communicate instructions for a particular action or set of actions. It carries information. Examples might

include instructions for building a piece of furniture or a toy; a map which sets out particular locations; diagrams, infographics and charts which convey statistical information; or photographs and images to accompany particular texts.

Children's author and illustrator, Benedict Blathwayt (2019), describes his relationship with maps:

> I always loved maps, the brown bits that show higher ground, the water –
> wondering whether it is swimmable, if you could sail a boat in it. Sat Navs
> and Google Maps are blinkered by our specific question and only answer
> the 'now' and miss the excitement entailed in laying out a map on the table
> when everything and anything is possible.

As an artist whose work is built around a sense of place – both in the natural and human worlds – Benedict's interest in maps as a form of functional visual literacy shows the way this can help to inspire the imaginative.

Aesthetic visual literacy

Aesthetic visual literacy carries cultural messages and values. For instance, fashion carries implicit comments around body shape, size and gender. Photography can provide a commentary on reality, construction and artifice. Art and sculpture will use form, composition, artistic technique, methods and material for aesthetic value and for implicit commentary around society and human experience. We also see this in architecture where different materials, designs and the use of space can be used to highlight societal development and the need and methods for creating shelter.

Author and illustrator of information texts, Stephen Biesty (2019), discusses the ways in which early encounters with architecture helped to inform his distinctive style of illustration and visual information text through his cross-section books:

> Over the years the thing that has most inspired me and made me want to
> draw has been visits to historic buildings. I remember as a child enjoying the
> physical experience of being inside medieval castles and cathedrals. It was
> the combination of immense scale, fine intricate details and the powerful
> atmosphere of the past that really captured my artistic imagination.

Likewise, Nestle Children's Book Prize Gold Award winning illustrator David Roberts started his career in fashion illustration and continues to be heavily influenced by this, both in the creation of his work and in his understanding and interpretation of the work of others.

> Fashion is a major influence on my work, it's the starting point in creating a character. I am always thinking, what would they wear? Clothes can be a huge part of capturing or describing personality, or it can just be enormous fun to dress up a character. I often look back at old family photos and use the clothes that I wore or my sister or mother or grandmother wore when illustrating my books. Historical costume is probably my favourite thing to illustrate. I immerse myself in the research and search the library or museums to find period pieces in a bid to get the details correct. Detail is so important, it's one of the things I love most when looking at other artists work.
>
> (Roberts, 2019)

Just as aesthetic visual literacy can play a role in inspiring creators, it can also inspire reading. Ali Mawle, director of education for Cheltenham Literature Festival, wrote guidance for the National Gallery on how to 'read' a painting (see below). Many of these techniques can be adapted to explore illustrations and act as a valuable bridge between the subject areas. The framework for encouraging consideration and discussion of art was developed to support children in close observation, gathering information and visual clues and cues to arrive at their own interpretation and emotional response to a work, revealing levels of understanding that are nuanced and considered.

How to read a painting

Looking
Jumping in
Children are invited to imagine they are jumping into a picture, exploring every detail imagining that they are able to experience the sights, sounds and sensations in the picture, thinking about who they might encounter and what they might want to ask them.

Taking eyes for a walk
Children are asked to use their eyes to 'walk' around a picture exploring the top, bottom, the things closest to them – those in the foreground – and

those furthest away – in the background all of the time thinking about the people and objects in the picture.

Responding
Illustrations carry an immediacy meaning that our responses can happen almost instantaneously with encountering them. Responses are based around what is shown in an image and also the techniques and methods of composition used in its creation. Responding is itself therefore a creative act, unpicking and yet using experience and imagination to draw together an interpretation. A significant element of response arises through empathy and when people find themselves inhabiting the inner world of a work, bringing to life the feelings and experiences of this.

Artwork itself can act as a stimuli, not only for children and young people, but also for authors and illustrators as Ruth Brown (2019) discusses below. She reflects on how an exhibition of Samuel Palmer's work inspired her to adapt her techniques and try a new form, 'reigniting' her 'creativity':

Several years ago, I went to a stunning exhibition at the British Museum of the work of Samuel Palmer, a nineteenth century English artist whom I have always admired. It was particularly wonderful to see in real life the collection of works called the Oxford Sepias – a series of exquisite, small pen and ink and gum arabic studies of English pastoral scenes. I have never been confident drawing with pen and ink, but fired with enthusiasm, I rushed along to the local art suppliers purchased sepia ink, mapping pens and gum arabic, in order to attempt 'my own' Samuel Palmer. I decided to draw a cat, because having drawn hundreds of cats in the past, at least I would have confidence in drawing the subject, if not in using the medium. The resulting drawing is called Samuel's Cat – and I loved every second of the process. But it remained a one-off. I returned to my 'normal' way of working and produced another book. Several years of upheaval passed, my husband died and I lost all desire to work. Eventually, to reignite my creativity, I decided to carry on the theme that I had started with Samuel and draw cats in the style of painters that I admire. At this stage I wasn't thinking in terms of a book so there was no pressure or deadlines and I was able to just get absorbed in the pure pleasure of working again. But the 12 paintings that I produced seemed to want to be a book and Sarah Pakenham of Scallywag Press, who I'd known and worked with at Andersen Press for almost 30 years, wanted to publish it, and with the invaluable help of Janice Thomson, my editor and long standing friend, it has indeed become a book, *The Gallery of Cats*. It has taken a while but that is often the case with ideas, some take ages to evolve while others, like *Ten Seeds*, arrived in my head fully formed. As a wonderful post script – a few years ago I was contacted by a professor William Vaughan who had written the definitive biography of Samuel Palmer called *Shadows on the Wall*. Through a long series of coincidences he had seen my Samuel and asked if he might include it in the book to illustrate a tailpiece that he'd written and called 'Samuel's Cat'. I was thrilled and extremely flattered, as you can imagine.

Narratological visual literacy

Narratological visual literacy is what Will Eisner termed 'sequential art' – the fact that images and pictures are capable of sustaining and progressing stories. There are numerous forms through which stories can be told in pictures and these offer a range of experiences. Forms include picturebooks, comic strips, graphic novels, manga or – when embracing moving images – films, animations, television programmes or computer games.

Former children's laureate, Lauren Child, discusses the role of visual literacy in her introduction to a British Council exhibition on illustration, *Drawing Words* (2018):

> In my view, illustration is widely misunderstood. There is a belief that the purpose of illustration is secondary, merely there to represent the world in pictorial form, but good illustration is so much more. A picture can convey a thought, a feeling, or an idea succinctly and exquisitely and, sometimes with more impact than a whole book full of words. A skilled illustrator can conjure vast landscapes and then, with a turn of the page, take you from the plains of New Mexico to a small room in New York city.

As Lauren implies, visual literacy has the power to transport us to different places and times. In this chapter, we've explored some of the different types and applications for visual literacy now and through history; Chapter 2 looks at the terms and language that aid discussion of the subject and help us better understand the stages and approaches involved in its creation.

The Big Picture: terminology for talking about and critiquing illustration

A challenge facing practitioners who wish to draw upon the potential of visual literacy as a tool for children's reading development, is that the language used to describe and discuss visual literacy is still being developed and has yet to be applied consistently upon the form. An interdisciplinary approach to assessing and understanding visual texts is useful for unpicking the method of creation and the layers of meaning implicit in visual texts. The disciplines drawn upon to form this lexicon include cultural studies, film studies, fine art, art theory, literature, design and production. The convergence of these areas allows us to communicate and impart an understanding of how visual texts work.

This chapter outlines the key terminology for discussion and appraisal of visual literacy and illustration, which is supported by a full glossary of terms appended to this book.

The building blocks for visual literacy

There are many aspects that come together to form a visual experience that conveys the message of a visual narrative. Each of these aspects may be employed individually, but often they will interrelate, creating a memorable and distinct impact upon the reader. The section that follows explores some of the core building blocks in the creation of a visual experience.

Illustration

Quantity of illustrations in a book may vary from as little as the cover illustration to the entire book being visual. Alongside titles where a synergy exists between words and pictures, there are also 'silent stories' that are comprised solely of images with no words. Illustration style, technique and media may vary substantially.

Describing the role of illustration in an interview for *ACHUKA*, three times winner of the Kate Greenaway medal and former children's laureate Chris Riddell (2007) states: 'good illustration is, by definition, illuminating and should add to the reader's enjoyment, stimulating their imagination – I refer you to [John] Tenniel, [Pauline] Baynes and Quentin Blake.'

Design
Design incorporates the typesetting and the layout of images and text on a page. Successful design can play a large role in how artwork is showcased and how the relationship between text and illustration operates; this is called compositional design and relies on a union where text and illustration are brought together in synergy to create unified meaning, this may be through complementary or contrasting elements of pictorial and written words.

Typography
Typography refers to the style and appearance of the text that is telling the story. It includes the use and choice of fonts and font size, as well as any typographical effects such as those that help to establish mood or intent, e.g. enlarged upper case fonts in speech bubbles to suggest SHOUTING! Or smaller text to indicate whispering.

Photography
Photos may be used to show real world examples of a person, place or time. These can be found in biographies, travel books and books detailing the natural world or scientific fact. Photographs can provide images as seen by the human eye, but can also enable close-ups, such as views of micro-organisms, or panoramics that would not be visible to the naked human eye, thus extending the field of vision. Photographs may also be used to convey an 'authentic' experience as is suggested by the maxim, 'the camera never lies'. Technology, however, can easily be manipulated or challenged subverting the expectations of 'truth' that viewers have.

Cinematography
Cinematography is the art of motion-picture photography and might be in the form of an animation or live-action film. The origins of moving pictures can be traced to zoetropes, a pre-film animation device that housed an inlaid reel of images, encased in a series of slits that when rotated at speed gave the appearance of movement. Cinematography tells

a story through a series of scenes that unfold to convey a particular message. Although an extensive media in its own right, elements of this can be recreated in printed form through flip-book animations which has been used to create illustrative details on the pages of children's novels, such as the *Jiggy McCue* books by author Michael Lawrence and illustrated by Ellis Nadler.

The anatomy of a picturebook

One of the challenges in discussing visual literacy is in drawing upon a language that can adequately describe and outline the processes that occur when we read visually. There are three stages in this:

1. The creation of the work and ways in which an impression is left which influences readership.
2. How this is decoded and the skills and processes involved in reading text and illustration simultaneously.
3. An understanding of how visual texts operate, this can help in selecting the very best titles for collections and in creating new texts with young people.

Well-constructed picturebooks have a definite make up or anatomy that not only helps to determine the way in which their story is told, it encourages reader interaction and exploration. Generally, picturebooks are made up of 32 pages or by a number that is divisible by eight. This is due to the way in which paper is printed. A 32-page picturebook can be printed onto one large piece of paper and then divided into pages – an efficient and cost-effective method of printing. These pages form the layout used to create the narrative structure and pace to the story. Picturebook author and illustrator, Jon Agee (2019), discusses the way he approaches picturebooks and the impact that layout can have on the telling of a story:

> Part of writing and illustrating a picture book involves figuring out the way you want to physically (graphically) present your story. Will it be the standard 32 pages? Does it need to be longer? Will it rely on a few big page turns, or many? Will it utilize single page spreads and double page spreads (where the picture crosses the gutter) or simply double page spreads

throughout? Will the story break the fourth wall? Will it ask the reader to interact? Will it incorporate text in the picture?

It's not enough to simply be a good illustrator, writer or designer. A picture book is about sequential images, the play of words and pictures, pacing, timing, scale, perspective, point-of-view, etc. Left and right page (verso and recto) can have distinct roles. Page turns can set up punch lines and surprises. There are a lot of things to consider, which is part of the reason I enjoy what I do.

These elements of discoverability that Jon refers to help to make the act of reading and engaging with a book more pleasurable and enticing for the reader.

Before readers immerse themselves in the story, they encounter the pages that appear before and after the story, which are known as the peritext. These are the images and textual elements that are secondary to the story and can be used to build anticipation and set the scene for the story and its subject, themes or mood or to develop them further.

Included in the peritext is the book cover. Cover images are usually the first element of a book to capture the attention of, or intrigue, potential readers. Cover imagery may be produced on dustjackets that adorn the book or printed on the cover of the book itself. Where dustjackets are used, removing these may uncover hidden visual elements that further convey the theme or atmosphere of the book.

It is important to consider the design and production decisions that have played a large role in the appearance of the cover of a book and its ability to capture the attention of potential readers. Choices made will include the overall image and any kind of special techniques employed to draw attention to aspects of the cover, such as, lamination, spot glosses, embossing, die-cut and foil blocking.

Lamination is the application of a thin layer of plastic which can visually enhance the cover design making colours appear more vibrant while protecting the print and making the book more durable. There are several types of lamination and each creates a different effect that impacts on readers. Gloss lamination is notable for its high sheen. Gloss can make images appear sharp and make contrasts appear more pronounced. Matte lamination has a smooth, softer finish. Matte often appears more natural and does not give the appearance of increasing contrast. Silk lamination results in a finish that, like matte, is natural looking but with a softer, more tactile finish that often gives the book an air of quality or sophistication.

Spot gloss, or spot UV is a technique that can enhance the visual experience of a cover. Printers will apply a gloss finish to a specific area of print, drawing emphasis to an element of the cover in the way the light hits the particular spot. This is often used to literally *highlight* book titles, main characters, or buildings to ensure that they stand out. The varnish used to create this affect is sealed using ultraviolet light, lending the technique its name. This technique has also been used to great effect in picturebooks about ghosts or invisibility such as Lauren Child's *Slightly Invisible*, where an absence is suggested by the story and enhanced by the subtle visual reference.

Embossing or debossing is a technique to retrospectively make elements of the cover stand out in relief, or else to appear concave. Both can create a more multi-dimensional appearance to an image. Likewise, both are techniques that are sometimes employed in board books, helping to give a more tactile element which can engage interaction with very young readers, or readers with learning needs.

Die-cut is a technique for cutting shapes and holes into books. It can create real impact on covers making them feel highly tactile. The die is a blade that has been formed into a particular pattern or shape, which is used to cut shapes or holes into the paper or board of covers. An example of this can be found on the hardback cover of Emily Gravett's Kate Greenaway winning title *Little Mouse's Big Book of Fears* where the appearance of a gnawed hole is positioned as part of the jacket design and behind which Little Mouse is sited. Die-cuts can be used to give interactive elements allowing small objects to be pushed through the hole or providing access to parts of the pages of the book that are to follow.

Foil blocking is a process whereby a metallic looking film is added to the surface of the paper. These films come in a variety of different shades, including gold, silver and various colours, and can also be holographic. Again, this technique can be used in book pages. When used in this way it is most commonly found in board books.

Turning the cover of a picturebook reveals pages that are attached to the cover – this occurs both with the front and back cover – these are termed endpapers. Traditionally endpapers were marbled or used coloured paper. In illustrated books, it has become common for these to feature illustrations that in some way draw on the theme or subject of the book. As the endpapers effectively bookend the book itself, sometimes these are adapted to show a change or shift that has occurred through the course of the story, for example, daytime may be depicted on the opening endpapers and a shift to night-time on the closing endpapers.

Although, as previously indicated, picturebooks tend to be comprised of 32 pages, the way these are structured can vary enormously – a testament to the innovation and imagination that can be brought to the picturebook format. Despite these variations, most will feature a title page and often have bibliographic details, or front matter. It is also common for the front matter to feature some form of illustration, often a vignette – a small isolated illustration without any form of border. This often foreshadows an element of the story or represents a part of the mood or atmosphere of the story that the reader can expect to encounter in the book. When sharing picturebooks, these isolated illustrations can provide a useful prompt to engage the audience, by asking them what or who they think the book might be about and what they feel might happen. Similarly, bibliographic details can be designed to visually reflect part of the story, perhaps being recreated in the image of a book, or in the form of a particular shape that has relevance to the story – like a love heart.

The pages that carry the main story are termed spreads. These are commonly stretched across two pages, termed double-page spreads. The compositional layout of a picturebook determines how the text and images work together. It may be that these are separate or integrated. Where integrated, if text overlays an image, it is often important to consider readability and how well the font colour and size contrast with the image. This is an especially important consideration for readers with visual impairments including colour blindness (see page 100). As part of the compositional layout, while contrast is key for readership, another core consideration is how well text and image cohere to provide a consistent visual experience. Left hand pages are termed as verso and right hand pages recto. In Western society, the convention is to read from left to right and to follow the sequence of pages accordingly. Visual information that happens in harmony can create a very natural flow, whereas that which goes right to left can create an impact that feels jarring or disorientating as though sawing against the grain in wood. As we observe in poetry, spreads can create a rhythm or a sequence with cause and effect, or set-up and consequence being shown. This can help to establish the pace of a visual story and aids the way in which the story can be read aloud and shared. This is particularly helpful for pre-readers (see page 43) to recognise and to follow the pattern of the plot.

The book itself is kept together by the process of binding. Readers will discover a line runs down the centre of each double-page spread where the pages are held together. This is called the gutter. It can be used compositionally to great effect separating elements of an image and highlighting opposing characters or factions. Where poor design choices are made without proper consideration of the gutters, this can result in key aspects of the illustration being lost from sight. In graphic novels, the gutter is extended to describe the space between individual panels and again can be used to great effect showing the movement between periods of time or geographic places.

The composition of a picturebook also uses the dimensions of the page to achieve affect in numerous ways.. Bleeds, for instance, allow the print of an image to extend to the furthermost reaches of the paper's edges – indeed the name itself derives from the fact that the printed edges often bleed off the paper. This gives illustrations an immersive quality drawing the audience in and can also suggest the scene is limited only by the audience's field of view, suggesting the world of the story extends beyond the page. A frame, on the other hand, is when an image does not reach the edge of the paper but instead blank space is left surrounding the image. It may be that several frames are held in sequence, these are then referred to as panels and usually denote a relationship that is either geographic, showing progression through a landscape or setting, or one which is temporal and shows the passage of time. These relationships are often critical to the dynamics of graphic novels. A single row of panels is called a tier. A splash is a large illustration that fills most of if not all of a page –this breaks the flow of panels and can make a real impact helping to establish a sense of place, time or mood.

As Jon Agee pointed out, the idea of the page turn is often an important part of how picturebooks function. These can operate as cliff-hangers to build suspense and anticipation before the image and text continue on the next page. Page turns can also be utilised to great effect when reading aloud and sharing a book, making use of dramatic pauses or intervening to ask the audience what they think might happen next! The build of anticipation can similarly be achieved between the panels in a graphic novel.

In some cases, illustrations closely match the language of the text, creating a visual representation of what is being described in the story but there may be divergences which allow the visual reader to see different elements or interpretations of the story. This is called counterpoint and can be described as the interpretative or imaginative space between the story as written and as shown in pictures.

The section that follows identifies various visual elements that contribute to the creation of this 'imaginative space' and the contributions colour can play in creating atmosphere and tone.

The role of colour

Colour can massively influence the responses we have to images. Scientifically speaking, colour is the result of the wavelengths of light which are visible to the eye. Sometimes known as chromatics, colour has a history of associations that vary according to culture and indeed individual readers. This means that colour palettes will have varying impacts upon visual readers. Illustrator Petr Horacek (2019) discusses how he uses colour and its importance to his artwork:

> I studied fine art and I have been painting all my life. Everything I know about colour I learned from painting outdoors. Colour is always important in my work. A good picture book needs a good rhythm. Definitely in the story and in the text. But, I believe, also in the colour atmosphere of the book. With colour, you can often say as much as you can say with the text itself. You can paint sadness or joy and happiness, cold, heat, any part of the day and more.

The role of colour can help to determine the mood of a book. Multi-award winning illustrator Oliver Jeffers (2019) describes colour as the 'third player' in the construction of his books:

> The way in which I approach colour in my art is mostly subconscious and instinctual. When conceiving an image in my head, the colour is usually there from the start and I rarely question it. How a particular palette got in my head to begin with, is probably from having seen the combination somewhere in real life, and stored it away – a moonrise over a valley, a piece of old packaging on a wood table, a detail of an old painting. Who knows. The general idea with inspiration is that you can never quite recall where a particular thing came from after it's been jumbled around inside you for however long. Sometimes though, what begins in the head doesn't translate

to paper, and in those cases, I am left with a sense of editing and judging as I go, reacting with what 'feels' right. What feels right, now that I think of it, is often one vibrant colour in a world of more muted colours of a similar hue. A normal pink will positively sing if it is the single flourish in a range of almost greys. And a colour that might look grey, when placed beside colours with only subtle differences, can suddenly become a deep blue, once the eye makes the connection between it and its environment. My most recent book, *The Fate of Fausto* is a good example of this – though the colour choices were initially born out of practical restriction from the traditional lithography press on which the art was made. The first half of the book – set on land – is made of deep umbers and tans, highlighted by a fluorescent red used sparingly. The second half of the book – set at sea – uses a range of dull cold blues, contrasted with a florescent yellow used exclusively for the characters rain mac, and the extremely subtle reappearance of pink toward the end as the flower he pinned to his lapel floats back to the surface. The use of colour in my book frequently becomes a third player to the composition of the images, and secondly the structure of the words. It can set an emotional tone without the reader being aware a tone is being set at all, allowing the composition and word use to be pushed further than they might be otherwise.

The importance of colour in the composition of picturebooks is undeniable. Indeed, colour has been identified as an essential part of illustration for hundreds of years. Recognising the need for a scientific methodology of drawing upon colours, Abraham Gottlob Werner compiled *Werner's Nomenclature of Colours* (1814) in an attempt to map 79 tints against selected examples from the animal, vegetable and mineral kingdoms. This historic text provides a benchmark against which colours can be assessed.

In describing an object, to specify its colour is always useful; but where colour forms a character, it becomes absolutely necessary. How defective, therefore, must description be when the terms used are ambiguous; and where there is no regular standard to refer to.

(Werner and Smye, 1814)

Werner captures here the vital and complementary role that images and colour plays alongside descriptive text.

It is important to note, however, that illustrations might be reproduced in monochrome – typically using one colour of ink as its base but presenting this in different shades to give density and form. This is common in black and white illustration, where the application of the medium (black) and the space of the 'canvas' (white) can be used to interact and interplay, creating striking, high-impact illustrations such as those seen in Jim Kay's Kate Greenaway medal winning illustrations for *A Monster Calls*, where the images convey the sense of brooding fear and isolation that the protagonist, Conor, experiences.

There is a range of terminology associated with colour which are considered in more detail below.

Hues are the different types of colour. They are determined by the wavelength of light that is received by the eye. In production terms, it is important that hues are matched exactly by the printer to best reproduce an illustration. A system of pantones is used for this which allow colours to be matched by specifying the ratio of four inks that compose the colour. These inks are cyan, magenta, yellow and black (CMYK).

Tone is the level of light or dark in a composition. Variations in tone can help to give the effect of light and shadow in an image.

Saturation is the level of intensity of a colour. Mixing hues with white lowers the saturation and creates a tint of the original hue.

There are whole sets of ideas around the impact and effects that colour can have upon people and the moods that they represent or evoke.

Illustrator Eva Eland (2019) discusses the way she uses colour and its association as a tool in figuratively carrying meaning:

> Paying close attention to composition, colour, body language and visual
> metaphors in picturebooks can uncover a lot of layers and subtleties that we
> might otherwise miss. Even if the illustrator didn't create all of these layers
> intentionally, all of us grew up with stories and images, be it in books or
> films we have watched, and even young children might already be able to
> contextualise many images and be better equipped at illustrating and
> interpreting illustrations than we might suspect.

The influence of colour can be seen across numerous aspects of daily life, from the interior design of homes and workspaces to print media and films. Colours play a particularly identifiable role in fairytales, where characters and emotions are vividly portrayed through colour association. Discussing the use of colours in fairytales, author Katherine Langrish (2014) states, 'colours in fairytales aren't decoration, they aren't even "just" descriptive. They carry information. They are a form of emphasis. And they can be relied upon.'

The section that follows uses the colour guidebook from *Werner's Nomenclature of Colours* (1814) to define various colours, citing the animal, vegetable and mineral Werner used to describe each colour and various other connotations that have come to be associated with them.

Charting colour

White

Snow white is the characteristic colour of the whites; it is the purest white colour; being free of all intermixture, it resembles new-fallen snow.

 Animal: breast of the black headed gull.

 Vegetable: snow-drop.

 Mineral: carara marble and calc sinter.

White is the Chinese element associated with metal.

 Scientifically, white is composed of all spectrums of light, as can be shown by refracting light through a prism where the wavelengths are separated. White includes a range of cultural associations which include purity, virginity, historical associations with death and with mourning – it is still used as shrouds and with chastity hence its use in marriage. White can lead to feelings of cold, or sparseness and has natural associations with snow.

 In fairytales, 'Snow White', is beautiful and pure.

Grey

Ash grey is the characteristic colour of Werner's greys; he gives no description of its component parts; it is composed of snow white, with portions of smoke and French grey, and a very little yellowish grey and carmine red.

 Animal: breast of long tailed hen titmouse.

 Vegetable: fresh wood ashes.

 Mineral: flint.

Grey is mixed of white and black pigments. It embraces cultural associations that include being tired or aged and ideas of indecision where items are described as being 'a grey area'.

Black

Velvet black, is the characteristic colour of the blacks; it is the colour of black velvet.

Animal: mole, tail feather of black cock.

Vegetable: black of red and black West Indian Peas.

Mineral: obsidian.

Black is the Chinese element associated with water.

Scientifically black represents a void of light, or the complete absorption of all light rays. Black has associations with death with 'black Mariah's', with darkness, with evil in Christianity, but also with warding off evil with the use of kohl to help stave it off. Historically black dye was produced from oak galls, but would fade quickly.

Blue

Berlin blue, is the pure, or characteristic colour of Werner.

Animal: wing feathers of jay.

Vegetable: hepatica.

Mineral: blue sapphire.

Blue is one of the primary colours. It has been said to be calming and soothing and carries associations of the sky and the sea. Blue also has associations with sadness when people are 'feeling blue', or upon 'Blue Monday', supposedly one of the most depressing days of the year in January, or when people sing the blues. Blue has religious associations with the Virgin Mary often being depicted in blue or Lord Krishna in the Hindu religion being blue skinned. It also has associations with royalty where one can be described as 'blue blooded'. Historically, blue was produced from indigo dye, although many pigments and dyes are now synthetic.

Purple

Campanula purple, is ultramarine blue and carmine red, about equal parts of each: it is the characteristic colour.

Animal: not applicable.

Vegetable: Canterbury Bell, Campanula Persicifolia.

Mineral: fluorspar.

Purple is a composite created from blue and red pigments. It has associations with creativity, fertility, magic and royalty. Its associations with royalty arise from the historical method of its production. Tyrian purple was created from crushed sea shells, it required thousands of sea shells to create. The method of its extraction led to a pungent pigment, so it was often perfumed. Purple prose also draws upon this royal association and is characterised by exaggerated or self-consciously grandiose or pompous wording.

Green

Emerald green, is the characteristic colour of Werner; he gives no description of the component parts of any of the characteristic colours; it is composed of about equal parts of Berlin blue and gamboge yellow.

Animal: beauty spot on wing of teal drake.

Vegetable: not applicable.

Mineral: emerald.

Green is the Chinese element associated with wood.

It carries associations with nature and particularly with growth etymologically the word derives from growan, meaning to 'grow'. It is the colour associated of Gaelic Ireland. In popular phraseology green is associated with envy with phrases like, 'green with envy' and the 'green eyed monster'. In folk-lore, the Green Man represents growth and regeneration and resultant qualities of stability and energy as in poet Dylan Thomas' poem, 'The force that through the green fuse, drives the flower.' Green is comprised of yellow and blue pigments.

Yellow

Gamboge yellow, is the characteristic colour.

Animal: wings of goldfinch, canary bird.

Vegetable: yellow jasmine.

Mineral: high coloured sulphur.

Yellow is the Chinese elements associated with earth.

Yellow carries associations with sunshine and energy and is known for being a stimulating colour. It is also a colour associated with cowardice, with terms like 'yellow belly'. In areas of Europe the colour is associated with envy, conditions like jaundice can mean that yellow is used to denote illness. Charlotte Perkins Gilman's *The Yellow Wallpaper*, showcases the way in which the colour is sometimes associated with emotional distress due to overstimulation. In history, the colour has been used as a symbol of Judaism with the Star of David reproduced in yellow, this was infamously the insignia used during the Holocaust. In Chinese culture yellow is often associated with gold and wealth. Yellow is one of the primary colours and historically was often created using lead-chromium oxide. This gave a brilliant yellow, but its lead content made it highly toxic. It was used to paint van Gogh's sunflowers and there are suggestions that it contributed to the mental health challenges he faced.

Orange

Orpiment orange, the characteristic colour, is about equal parts of gamboge yellow and arterial blood red.

Animal: the neck ruff of the golden pheasant, baby of the warty newt.

Vegetable: Indian Cress.

Mineral: not applicable.

Orange is a blend of red and yellow pigments. It has associations with the sun, warmth and is a colour that stimulates. Its high visibility means it is used to signify importance and so it can be found on traffic cones, high visibility vests and more. Orange means 'fragrant', the name derived from Sanskrit narangah the fruit and the pungent citrus oils contained in its peel. Religiously the colour has ties with Buddhism and Hari Krishna. The dye was created from saffron.

Red

Arterial blood red, is the characteristic colour of the red series.

Animal: head of the cock gold-finch.

Vegetable: corn poppy, cherry.

Mineral: not applicable.

Red is the Chinese element associated with fire.

Red is one of the primary colours. Culturally it is a colour that is often associated with significance, as can be shown by 'red letter days', on calendars, the dates that were significant, religious dates or holidays. As with yellow and orange, red is highly stimulating. Red also has associations with blood, fertility and birth rites, with fire and death. It also has ties with luck and celebration (in part due to body adornment paint). In Christianity, it has ties with evil and is often symbolic of the 'fire and brimstone' of hell. Red is frequently depicted as a colour associated with passion, aggression and rage. Politically the colour red is often associated with the Left and with ideas of communism.

The fairytale character 'Red Riding Hood' makes appearances across a wide range of cultures.

Brown

Chestnut brown, the characteristic colour of the browns of Werner's series, W. is deep reddish brown and yellowish brown.

Animal: neck and breast of red grouse.

Vegetable: chestnuts.

Mineral: Egyptian jasper.

Brown is often associated with nature and the earth. There are a wide range of shades. The colour often has military overtones due to its use in camouflage uniforms, it was the colour used by the 'Brown Shirts' in Nazi Germany.

Media, style and techniques

Having considered the structure, composition and design choices that go into the production of picturebooks, the remainder of this chapter explores the media, style and techniques used by artists to create an impact on the reader. Human ingenuity means there are a range of different media that can be used to create illustrations. Argentinian illustrator, Gusti, is a good example of this. In his picturebook, *Half of an Elephant*, (2006) the eponymous elephant is formed out of all manner of commonly discarded items – buttons, screws, paintbrushes, cardboard, even slices of bread – to create zany, irreverent illustrations full of energy and humour. Use of these commonplace materials can inspire and encourage children to create their own illustrations, stimulating ways of seeing the world through a different lens.

Other artistic media include:

Printmaking – including linocut, woodcut, etchings and monoprints. Multiple layers give depth and can create copies that are almost facsimiles with variations occurring in how the print media is used. This differs from a reproduction in that the artist has directed the creation of the copy through every stage from conception to execution. The number of copies in a run of prints is called an edition and traditionally these are often signed and numbered. There are four main types of printmaking, relief printmaking, intaglio printmaking, lithographic printing and screenprinting. Further information on each can be found in the glossary appended to this book.

Drawing – the apparatus or media used may include pencils, charcoal, pens (with various inks) or pastels. Use of line is important in drawing, this might be loose, giving the appearance of spontaneity, energy and free-spiritedness. They might also be more formal where the artist has tried to recreate scale and accuracy of appearance. This is important in draughtsmanship and architecture. Drawing is often used in the creation of storyboards and roughs where illustrators are outlining the plot and pace of their visual stories. Common techniques include hatching, cross-hatching and stippling, further information on media and techniques can be found in the glossary.

Painting – the technique of using pigments on a canvas or paper to create an image. The method of application, brushes, sponges or spatula can affect the finished appearance. There are numerous types of paint including watercolours, acrylics and oil paints. Common techniques include underpainting, blocking in, texturising, sgraffito, drybrushing, washes, stippling, splattering, sponging, impasto and scumbling. Further information on these can be found in the glossary.

Photography – photographic images are created when an image is focused via the camera's aperture, onto a material which is light-sensitive (a film). Traditionally, this would be treated with chemicals, or developed, in order to reproduce the image. Zoom, perspective and colour saturation can be manipulated through use of different lenses and it is possible to double-expose film to give different effects, often lending the appearance of ghostly or ethereal apparitions. Photographs are now often taken digitally, again the image is focused via the aperture and technology within the camera captures this and converts it into electric signals storing this as millions (mega) of pixels.

Digital scans – similar to photographs, these allow the reproduction of various items and materials. Scanning is also commonly used to reproduce artwork itself allowing digital manipulation to take place, where artwork can be altered without endangering the finished work.

Mixed media – composite images constructed from a range of different artistic media. This might include photography, collage and hand drawn items. It can create a vibrant, visually rich experience.

Collages – an accessible way to encourage children to use materials from the world around them to create impactful pictures. Find out more from artist Jeannie Baker on page 34.

Papercut – images drawn together using cut pieces of paper. This may be in the form of cut-out images which form silhouette overlays above traditional illustrations, a form Jan Pienkowksi used regularly, or it might be through the layering and assembly of individual papercut elements as in the work of Caldecott Medal winning illustrator David Wisniewski.

Sculpture – this is three dimensional artwork; where used for illustration it is usually photographed. See, for example, *The Singing Bones* by Shaun Tan, where Grimm's fairytales are reimagined through sculpture.

Fabric – illustrations can be produced with fabric, for the creation of soft books, for example, material is used instead of paper. Fabric is commonly used for tactile books. Fabric and stitching can also be used and then scanned in to create illustrations for print books. Find out more from artist, Clare Beaton on page 35.

Style – there are patterns in terms of how particular artists use their media and techniques to portray their vision or subject matter. Many artistic styles can be grouped together in particular movements that are characterised by trends, or tropes, in much the same way as genres of literature. Many illustrative styles draw upon traditions associated with various artistic movements.

Naturalism – the artist attempts to paint objects realistically as they are seen and experienced in the everyday world. Naturalism shows human emotions. It endeavours to show light and texture in ways that are familiar and convincing.

Romanticism – a style based around the way mood and emotion can influence perception. In many ways it was a counter movement against the conventions of high art, seeking to embrace a freer more psychological perspective. The movement placed great emphasis around nature and landscape. Romanticism was a movement that worked across many areas of the arts – music, visual arts and writing.

Realism – much like Romanticism, this forms something of a counter movement to the conventions of high art whereby Biblical figures or those from mythology often formed the subject and iconography of artwork. Realism sought to place focus upon the common man in pursuit of everyday activities. As a movement, it rejected idealisation and often depicted scenes of working-class life, drawing focus on all aspects of this with an openness and honesty that was initially viewed as quite shocking.

Impressionism – this style also sought to reflect everyday life, often the outdoors captured spontaneously. Impressionists aimed to quickly capture the essence, or impression of a scene, showing the effects of light and darkness. The movement is characterised by free brushstrokes and often bright colours.

Pointillism – developed out of French painter, Georges Seurat's interest in the nature of colour and how this is perceived by the eye. Pointillism grew out of these theories of colour make-up and involves the artist applying paint in small isolated dots or points. From a distance and cumulatively, these dots form a picture and merge to give the illusion of a wide spectrum of colours.

Surrealism – the surrealist movement explores the unconscious mind and its effect on thoughts and dreams. In surrealism, the logical is often rejected in favour of free association and spontaneity. The influence of the movement can be found in works by illustrators such as Chris van Allsburg, Anthony Browne and David Wiesner.

Photorealism – rejecting the painterly qualities such as brushstrokes via which the creation of a piece of artwork can be discerned. As the name suggests, the movement sought to create images that looked almost photographic with a great sense of clarity. Subjects often include urban landscapes and still lifes.

Pop art – drawing inspiration from popular culture, pop art rejected some of the traditions of art in favour of reflecting the types of imagery and culture that artists saw around them. It questioned ideas of creation, construction and reproduction raising questions around the boundaries of what could be considered art and what could not.

Using other media in practice

Multi award-winning author and illustrator, Jeannie Baker (2019), describes the intricate collages she creates for her detailed illustrations and how these have served as a catalyst for children to create their own images:

> I receive countless emails and images from teachers very proud of the collages their children have created from a diverse range of collected materials in response to my books. Many respond to *Window* and *Belonging* with collage images from a window telling the story of changes to their own neighbourhood. Sometimes the collages created are enormous, the children working together as a group and each creating a detail within the whole.
>
> I've received many emails from teachers inspired by *Mirror*, telling me their class is working with a class in another very different part of the world that they have links with and that each child will create their own collage to

contribute to showing a typical school day and all the collages will work together to create the story of two children's days.

Jeannie also received feedback from educators about the impact of her illustrated books on young readers:

'They made remarkable connections that I thought were way beyond their scope.'

'Your books manage to leave the reader to pause and reflect amidst the chaos and to consider the things of true importance.'

'I love your work for the conversations it has started between the children and myself.'

Similarly, Clare Beaton (2019) explains how she uses fabric in her work and how she has engaged children in this form. Clare utilises different kinds of needlework, stitching and materials to compose her images, she provided an insight into her style and technique:

I have written and illustrated a variety of books for young children and feel that books are a vital part of their development. For me reading books to my children was one of the most enjoyable parts of being a mother. Happily, this is now being repeated as a grandmother.

I have illustrated picturebooks in handstitched fabric collage, using my collection of vintage fabrics, buttons and all manner of bits and pieces. I think the work appealed as friendly and homely with children counting the buttons and trying to feel the texture of the materials. Creating mermaids with sequined tails, dinosaurs with beaded armour and trees with shoelaces for trunks, intrigued children when I did readings or workshops showing original artwork. They could also make their own pictures using all the stuff I used but gluing instead of stitching.

I always add 'hidden' items and extra elements to the pictures over and above that necessary to the story so there was more to find and talk about.

I have also written and illustrated 100s (latterly in paper collage) of books combining facts and craft ideas. These are simple, fun projects clearly explained, recycling materials such as card tubes, encouraging children to get creative.

The best thing people sometimes tell me is that one of my books was loved by their children and has been kept over the years. How wonderful to have been part of someone's childhood!

Features of visual narratives

In addition to drawing upon elements from art, design and production, there are numerous conventions which are useful both for creating and for understanding how visual storytelling or narration works. These are outlined below.

Foreground – the objects or subjects found in the front portion of an image.

Background – the objects or subjects found in the rear portion of an image. These can help set scenes.

Midground – generally this is the part of an image that the eye is drawn to first. Often images make use of triangles in the composition of images or objects as these help to draw the eye further; this might be in the formation of a house roof or the positioning of eyes and mouth on the face of a character.

Establishing shot – commonly used in films, as the name suggests this is the image that opens a work. It can play an important role in literally setting the scene for where the story or action happens, or figuratively by foreshadowing some of the key themes, mood or subject matter. It is not uncommon for this to be used as part of a title page in picturebooks.

Recto – the formal term for a page on the right hand side of a publication.

Verso – the formal term for a page on the left hand side of a publication.

Perspective or point of view – this is the focal point from which the audience sees what is being depicted. It can have a surprising impact on the experience the reader has. An aerial perspective can give a bird's eye view of what is happening, providing a sense of how the geography of a place interlocks and relates. Seeing action unfurl from a child's eye perspective can often create a sense of union between child characters and the reader.

Eye level – use of perspective which is at eye level and which can create an intimacy between focal characters and the reader.

High angle – provides a higher angle giving the reader the experience of looking down onto a particular scene or circumstance.

Low angle – provides a lower angle giving the reader the experience of looking up on a particular scene or circumstance.

Graphic weight – this is the use of light and dark toned images or patterning to draw the eye to particular images that might carry significance in the overall picture.

Fade – a technique where an image is blurred and fades out to suggest either a change of focus or the end of a particular sequence.

Pan – through use of panels, graphic novels are often able to shift the focus across a particular vista or landscape.

Panorama – this replicates a photographic panorama which shows a broad view of a particular scene. This can be achieved by using the length of a tier of panels to show a single view.

Close up – a close up or macro, is an image that draws the viewer's attention to the object of focus in a heightened level of detail, as though it was literally being examined immediately before the eye.

Flashback – use of images that carry the reader back from the main narrative to a previous point. This can be achieved through the use of different colour palette – often black and white or sepia are used to show the shift.

Motif – this is a recurring visual which gives a weight of significance to a particular theme or subject. It may be that this is an illustrative element such as, a particular character, recurring leaves to suggest the passing of the seasons, or it may even be a single colour whose use suggests a tonal mood change.

Cross cutting – when a sequence in a narrative crosses over with that of another.

Cut-outs or Vignettes – illustrations which do not have a border. They are often used decoratively to break up text and are a common feature on title pages and the pages with bibliographic data.

Features in graphic novels

Graphic novels often have particular features and conventions. Some of the most frequently found are detailed below. It becomes increasingly common that these are cross-fertilised into the picturebook field.

Speech bubbles – also known as speech balloons, these are a convention for relating direct speech. The manner in which the bubble is produced can denote the force or volume of the speech. A dotted bubble indicates a character is whispering, whilst a spikey outline suggests shouting or screaming. Positioning of multiple bubbles can show the sequence in which dialogue occurs between characters. The thickness of the bubble's line can also indicate volume. Sizing and placement of speech bubbles in relation to one another can suggest power relations between the characters engaged in conversation.

Thought cloud – these are used to show the thought or interior monologue of characters. They are usually shown as a chain of clouds ascending from the character subject. In manga a fuzzy thought cloud is sometimes used where the thought occurs in a roughly circular shape with numerous intersecting lines to suggest the fuzziness of thought.

Captions – these are common in graphic novels and carry narration or the voice over, elements of necessary written story progression that are not direct speech and which might indicate the progression of time, a shift in place or in scene.

Visual explosions – sometimes called word bubbles, these are jagged shapes that often contain onomatopoeic sounds and are conventionally often used in fight scenes. These might include dramatic phrases such as 'Kapow', 'Thud', 'Bam!' The words themselves are often reproduced in fonts or hand-lettering that carries additional weight or size to help create drama and impact that immediately capture the eye.

Grawlix – used particularly in graphic novels, these are the use of font symbols *@#! in place of expletives. The word was coined satirically by American comic strip writer Mort Walker but caught on as a means of describing a convention within the form. Mort later wrote *The Lexicon of Comicana*.

Plewd – these are the, conventionally, teardrop shaped beads of sweat shown disseminating from a character and often used to denote heat, anxiety or stress. This is another term that was devised by Mort Walker.

Squeans – the stars that circle a character to indicate dizziness, intoxication or having suffered a blow to the head. A term devised by Mort Walker.

Movement lines – these are lines on an object or character which indicate force, momentum and often direction of travel.

Emanata – lines around a character's head to suggest a feeling of surprise. A term devised by Mort Walker.

Text box – as the name suggests a box within which text appears on a page, these can be used to contain the main narrative or might be used as break out boxes where additional information or asides are provided.

This chapter concludes with consideration of how the principles and ideas associated with illustration and visual literacy can stimulate children to make their own books. I spoke with two creators about their approach to visual storytelling; discussing his creative process, illustrator Benedict Blathwayt (2019) shared an insight into how he structures and plans his ideas for a story:

> I begin by writing down the story in scribbled text usually using biro. I divide this into the number of pages – usually 12 spreads – and create a mini storyboard (about the size of a matchbox), in fine sharp pencil. This is how I test to find whether the continuity and run works. If approved by a publisher, I will then create full size roughs where I makes all the mistakes of composition. The next stage is placing the roughs onto a homemade copylight. I then copy these onto watercolour paper before colouring them.

Illustrator, Laurence Anholt (2019), spoke about the pleasure to be found in creativity and expression when reconnecting with our innate curiosity and overcoming self-criticism and doubt, key areas when encouraging the creation of visual literacy:

> One of the main things I have learned about great artists is that they were not necessarily born with a natural graphic ability. Many, like Cézanne and van Gogh, were pretty clumsy. The reason they succeeded is because they did not let their self-doubts prevent them from realising their vision. It's the same with writing, and almost anything in life. In the end, we simply have to suspend our self-criticism and get stuck in. Very quickly, we find that creativity is fun, and it's actually the quirks and idiosyncrasies of what we produce that make it unique and interesting. Creativity is about being *ourselves*, rather than a false idea of what others want us to be. Remember, we were all artists as children – it was only when self-consciousness set in that our creativity began to dry up. The joy of creativity returns when we reconnect with our inner child.

The case study that follows shows young people putting their creativity into practice as they set about making their own book.

Case study 2.1   Make a Book

The lure of expression and creativity can be one that entices less confident and keen readers to actively engage with books, stories, information and reading. In Slough, Antonia Gray devised a 'Make a Book' project working in collaboration with a local school for children with special needs. The target age of participants was children aged between eight and nine years old (year four). The group included two girls and eight boys who were pre-literate.

The children involved in Slough's 'Make a Book' project favoured kinaesthetic learning, discovering through practical application and hands-on activity. Illustration provides rich opportunities for this. Aims for the project were that it should be accessible for all children, have clear outcomes and provide lasting value. Making a book was selected as the focus for the project. Antonia chose to base this around Emily Gravett's *Meerkat Mail* where a young meerkat visits relatives sending postcards home.

Using this visual story as a catalyst, children were encouraged to learn about different countries that the bear in their own story, Growly, might visit. Children were encouraged to write about the different places the bear had travelled writing a simple sentence and illustrating this with a picture, e.g. 'Growly visited Australia' with a picture of a kangaroo.

Small photographs from magazines and travel brochures were provided and used by the children to help illustrate the book. Through working independently on their own pages and as a group to form the book as a whole, children developed social and motor skills.

The school's curriculum leader stated, 'the act of creating a book and sharing it with their peers and carers is a far more interactive and experiential one than simply listening to a story being read aloud. Our pupils are largely kinaesthetic learners; they learn by doing. It is projects like this that spark interest in books as stories or as sources of information.'

The project led to improved links between the school and the library and teachers have subsequently expressed interest in bringing students to the library. The project received substantial media local media attention as well as being featured in CILIP's *Update* magazine.

CHAPTER 3

The Reading Journey: the developmental stages of reading

An understanding of the development of reading and readers is useful context for librarians, educational practitioners and parents alike. This chapter outlines current theories around how reading skills are developed and the common stages associated with this.

Reading is the process via which meaning is inferred and constructed from written text (Vellutino et al., 2004). There are three aspects required for fluent reading (Commodari, 2017): comprehension – how words themselves are understood; accuracy – the ability to read with precision; and speed – the time taken to decode words. The development of reading skills is predicated upon a number of factors meaning it is difficult to determine standard milestones. Access to learning and ultimately attainment is dependent upon core reading skills.

It can be easy to mistake acquisition of literacy with reading itself. Reading is an activity with several motivations, including learning and self-improvement, challenging ourselves, reinforcing and affirming existing ideas and knowledge, and the all-important reading for pleasure. A part of learning how to read is not just sequential progression, but also includes re-reading and exploring a range of materials and forms that might fall beneath the reader's current ability level, but nonetheless allows the discernment of different styles and techniques. This is often what makes reading a desirable pastime as opposed to simply being a skill that is held.

As children learn, it is important not to solely emphasise progressing through complexity of language and construction. Natural reading habits also include re-reading and exploring a range of materials and forms that may well fall below an individual's ability level but that nonetheless allow the discernment of different styles and techniques.

Visual literacy in particular often relies on a slower, more careful reading style. In order to extract detail and understanding, readers should take time to consider the levels and layers at work, to recognise the different patterns and references, and to appreciate the choice of style, construction and composition that can influence meaning. Caldecott winning illustrator, David Wiesner (2012), describes the way reading pictures forms a vital and multi-levelled approach to reading:

> Before they read words, children are reading pictures. In picture books, the pictures work in concert with the text in a way that is unique among art forms. Picture books tell stories in a visual language that is rich and multi-levelled, sophisticated in its workings despite its often deceptively simple appearance. It is through the book's images that a child understands the world of the story – where it is set, when it takes place, whether it's familiar or new. They read the characters' emotions and interactions in facial expressions and body language. There may be secondary pictorial storylines happening alongside the main action, like a secret for the child to notice and follow.
>
> This visual reading is as important to a child's development as reading written language. Take away the pictures and you deprive kids of a wealth of understanding – not to mention a lot of fun.

The growth and development of the aptitude to read visual texts is aligned with the development of the human eye as will be discussed further in this chapter. The human eye is a remarkable piece of apparatus. Light is focused by the cornea, this is the clear surface on the front of the eye, which acts as a protective layer. The iris controls the amount of light received through the dilation and un-dilation of the pupil. Towards the back of the eye is the retina. This is light sensitive and is able to convert optical images into electrical signals. These signals are transmitted to the visual cortex in the brain via optic nerves. Receiving signals from two eyes means that the brain is able to determine depth perception thereby allowing the relative size and distance of objects we encounter to be assessed. As a consequence of this, a full colour image can be registered and processed by the brain in a fraction of a second (Lindstrom, 1994).

Visual literacy thus has an immediacy not present in non-visual forms of art and communication. Author and academic, Morag Styles (2019), talks about the unique role and reading experience that visual narratives provide:

Most children are sophisticated readers of picturebooks as our research in the two editions of *Children Reading Pictures/Picturebooks* (2003/2016) confirms. The most appealing picturebooks form the primary literature of early childhood and offer many of the same delights as art objects. When they are engaged with absorbing picturebooks, children are able to make sense of complex images on literal, visual, affective and metaphorical levels, to understand different viewpoints, and analyse moods, messages and emotions. Children as young as four can either articulate or through drawing, demonstrate, deep personal responses to this powerful multimodal literature, if they find the book rewarding, amusing and stimulating. Even with all the exciting digital gadgetry around, picturebooks are more than holding their own because of the unique experience for children they provide (and the adults who read alongside).

Professor Maryanne Wolf, visiting Professor of Education at UCLA and Director of the UCLA Centre for Dyslexia, argues in her book *Proust and the Squid* (2008) that there are five distinct phases in the development of reading. A skill that she suggests is a cultural invention. The five stages of reading development can be categorised as follows:

1. The emerging pre-reader, this phase typically occurs between the ages of 6 months and 6 years.
2. The novice reader, this phase typically occurs between the ages of 6 and 7 years.
3. The decoding reader, this phase typically occurs between the ages of 7 and 9 years.
4. The fluent, comprehending reader, this phase typically occurs between the ages of 9 and 15 years.
5. The expert reader, this phase typically occurs from the age of 16 years and above.

These five stages provide a useful structure through which to explore the psychological steps involved with developing reading skills. Visual literacy can support and enhance reading at every stage of development, enabling access to a range of different information in accessible means.

The emerging pre-reader
The development of sight is an important factor for emerging pre-readers.

Newborn babies see basic shapes and can discern light and movement, but this is in grey and black and white only as colours are not yet differentiated. At this early stage in a child's development, eyes cannot yet be fixed on objects and tend to wander. The focal range for newborns tends to be between 20 and 30cm.

For the emerging pre-reader, board books are a key resource in early encounters with books and reading. The fundaments of looking – getting used to the book as an object, turning pages, holding attention and focus – can all be valuably experienced through board books. These can help to provide a familiarity, appetite and early aptitude for reading.

Black and white photographs are known to hold particular appeal for very young babies. Before eyes are functioning fully, when they are not able to discern between colours and when focal range is limited, the ability to differentiate between light and dark exists. Board books with simple bold black and white images are ideal to engage with at this age and can help with distinguishing basic concepts like patterns and shapes. In addition to helping support an early aptitude for reading, sharing books from an early age aids bonding, helping to nurture safe and healthy attachments between young children and their parents, guardians and care-givers.

Between the ages of one and two months, babies begin to focus both eyes on objects close to them. They are able to follow objects but their eyes are still likely to wander and are not fully under control. Differentiation of colours begins to occur with reds, oranges, yellows and green. Brightly coloured books can support early vision at this stage. At age three months vision begins to get much sharper. The eyes can focus upon objects more easily and accordingly babies can begin to track objects. These visual skills can be supported through sharing board books, pointing out different objects for the baby to focus upon.

By around five months shades of colour are able to be discerned more easily and a sense of depth perception is growing. As vision stabilises, fine motor functions begin to develop with increased hand-eye co-ordination. This can be a good age to make use of tactile elements that encourage interaction. Board books that use touch and trails are particularly useful allowing young readers to interact through starting to 'follow the course of a book' with their fingers, finding how pages turn and so actively progressing through sequential art.

At around seven months and above, babies will have clear enough vision to recognise people more easily. Board books with mirrors can help to support self-identification. By the time babies reach their first year, their sight is similar to that in adulthood with the ability to recognise objects at a distance and see things clearly and in focus.

Board books require a particular skill to create and produce. Many are produced in-house or are adaptations of existing picturebooks. Author and illustrator Petr Horacek (2019) describes some of the approaches he has taken to the board books he has created:

> *Strawberries are Red* is my very first published book. It is a board book about colours and fruit. The idea that a child may try to find out how it is that all the colours suddenly appear on the last page makes me smile.

> *Where Do You Live Snail?* is a board book about different kinds of animals and about the variety of the world we live in. The last page of the book has a turning wheel so that you can send the snail to 'bed'. It gives an idea that it was a snail's journey through the day. It makes the book rather cosy.

Figure 3.1 *A selection of board books for pre-readers by Petr Horacek*
© Petr Horacek, 2019

The early years, or emerging pre-reader stage in a child's development is fundamental in nurturing a love of books and reading. Awareness of this led to the founding of Bookstart, a programme started in the UK by Wendy Cooling. Bookstart was the world's first national book-gifting programme. It aimed to encourage and instil a love of books, stories and rhymes in children from an early age. Still running today, every child in England and Wales is gifted a free Bookstart pack before they are twelve months old and again between the ages of three and four. Find out more at www.booktrust. org.uk/what-we-do/programmes-and-campaigns/bookstart.

The Bookstart scheme has a number of key messages that are summarised below.

- Cementing the fact that parents and carers are children's first and most important teachers. Reading and sharing stories, books and rhymes are an essential part of early children's development and facilitate foundations skills that will aid them as they become confident, curious learners. Using pictures to explore parts of the story and to ask basic questions such as 'can you see the duck' is a valuable part of this 'sharing experience.'
- Encouraging the use of stories, books and rhymes from an early age. Babies might not understand the words, but will enjoy hearing the sound of the human voice and the timbre of this as well as being able to look at the illustrations.
- Sharing books, talking about pictures and being close together helps to build strong and secure relationships with all family members.
- Children benefit and enjoy all manner of books and enjoy making their own choices, libraries are a good way of facilitating this and giving children free choice.
- Babies love books which feature bright, bold pictures and photographs.
- That making time to share books together every day is quality time that can be spent together and contributes to children's early learning and development.

Silent stories, picturebooks that do not have words, but nonetheless encourage the advancement of a story or information journey through the progression of pages in the book, can be a useful means for independently developing the physical faculties which are the basis for reading. Positive affirmation is incredibly important to aid motivation and engagement in reading and silent stories and picturebooks allow emergent readers to practice reading fundaments as they see modelled by readers around them.

Continuing to share stories reinforces this modelling and gives opportunities for observation and construction of the story message. The illustrations in some picturebooks lend a different interpretation to the story itself, allowing emerging readers to experience the satisfaction of inferring meaning from the visual text.

Key concepts that help emerging readers to better familiarise themselves and make sense of their world and experiences can be supported and cemented through ongoing access to books with visual images that reflect the world and life experiences of young children. This can support early learning through communication and language.

As young children begin to recognise patterns in letter sounds, they can be supported through helping to recognise letters of the alphabet, associating these with word sounds. Illustrated alphabet books can be an invaluable way to start to introduce the relationship between letter shapes and the sounds and the words they are associated with. These can be in book form, or might take the form of flashcards which can be used to aid learning through play. Illustrated nursery rhymes are also useful to help increase vocabulary, illustrations can help to make these accessible and act as aide memoirs supporting memorisation and early aptitude for literacy.

Former children's laureate and multi award-winning illustrator, Anthony Browne, discusses Evelyn Arizpe and Morag Styles' research into children's responses to contemporary picturebooks, *Children Reading Pictures*:

> When I first read *Children Reading Pictures*; I found it intensely moving. I was deeply touched by the children's response to *Zoo* and *The Tunnel* …The children's sophisticated reactions didn't surprise me as I've known for some time how we often undervalue the abilities of children to see and understand…They were able to pick up on themes and ideas that I hadn't expressed in the text, only in the pictures. Children are wonderful readers of visual metaphors…This book, I think proves beyond doubt children's innate ability to derive true meaning from pictures.
>
> (Browne cited in Arizpe and Styles, 250, 2003)

This ability of young readers to discern meaning from picturebooks can also benefit their early understanding of their bodies and physical activity. Illustrations of the body in picturebooks, such as Zita Newcombe's *Toddlerobics* or Fearne Cotton's *Baby Yoga*, can help children to recognise and learn parts of the body and develop a sense of understanding of their own movement.

Picturebooks can also introduce concepts around basic mathematics using some of the rudimentary language combined with visual representations of numbers through illustration. Counting books are an ideal way to do this and allow picture readers to count out the number of objects depicted in the illustrations. A study to identify the importance of reading in introducing young children to mathematics (Mix et al., 2012) found that 69% of spontaneous utterances made by parents when reading a counting book were numerical in nature. This linguistically increases the likelihood of exposing early years children to language useful for basic numeracy. Whether in counting books or not, asking children to count the number of items or animals in a picture offers an interactive way to practice counting.

Through illustrated books, emerging pre-readers can be introduced to and explore a range of different disciplines.

The novice reader

At the stage when readers are novice, they are beginning to connect the relationship between letters when written, and sounds when spoken. They are able to read simple texts and they will have an increasing aptitude in recognising and sounding out words. A reader's comprehension at this stage is likely to be above their decoding skills meaning that they are better able to understand the themes or subject of a book or story when read aloud than they would be able to infer from their own reading of a text. This evidences that, at this stage, there is still great benefit in reading aloud.

Reading can be encouraged and enhanced by providing opportunities for practice in a non-pressured and non-time restricted way. Finding opportunities to continue sharing stories will also help to build a love of reading. Developing aptitudes in visual literacy will also help young readers to recognise sight words.

There are a variety of visual reading materials which can assist readers at the novice stage of development. A selection of these are explored below.

Picturebooks – these might include simpler texts to practice reading independently and more sophisticated texts which can be shared. Illustrations can help in outlining the relationship between words and their meaning. However short, picturebooks can engage with challenging and complex issues as Jon Agee (2019), author and illustrator of *The Wall in the Middle of the Book* explains:

Many picture books explore important issues that affect society. Among Dr Seuss's books, he covered racism, environmentalism, and nuclear war. Maurice Sendak's *We're All in the Dumps with Jack and Guy* was inspired by a photograph of homeless children in Brazil. John Burningham's *Aldo* seems to be about a girl whose parents have separated. In William Steig's *Amos and Boris*, a mouse, fearing he's about to drown in the ocean, talks candidly about mortality.

Comics – the printed comic industry has seen a decline over the past two decades with the fall of the Fleetway group whose stable included titles like *Whizzer and Chips, Buster, Cor, Oink* and many more. In 2012, *The Dandy* printed its final paper-based issue and became an online publication; this however was not viable and the publication ceased altogether within six months. Despite this, comics are a useful reading tool; the panels contain large scale visuals and the stories are driven in the main by short, snappy dialogue making for fast-paced reads. The fact that many strips are humorous or action-packed makes them pleasurable to read and means there is a sense of achievement and accomplishment on completion of a strip. Making comics available as part of the library offer and even organising a swap box where children can exchange issues of their favourite comics can be a useful and low-cost way of helping to ensure provision is made. For more ideas around comics, see Chapter 4 (pages 79–83).

Illustrated first readers and chapter books – these can be very useful for novice readers as they have a good sense of pace between chapters and include illustrations that help to support the reading and break up the text to create an engaging way to explore aspects of the story.

Visual note taking – this is a useful way of recording information in a visual context. Visual note taking can allow different inter-relationships to be made clear, discernible and memorable. It can be a way of recording and making information accessible before children have acquired full literacy skills

Founder of the publishing company Cicada Books, Ziggy Hanaor (2019), considers the relationship children have with images throughout their development, particularly at the pre-literate stage:

> We live in a world that is packed with visual indicators, and children are absolute masters at reading those signs and interpreting them. I think the pre-literacy stage is quite magical. It's a bit like losing one of your senses and your other senses making up for that loss. Children who are unable to read have an acute ability to understand images. When literacy kicks in, images and words become equal in value, and finally words take over. I love the way children interpret images and fill in the gaps in the story with those interpretations.

The decoding reader

Key characteristics for the decoding stage of reader development is that readers will be able to read simple and familiar stories and selections with increasing fluency. As listening comprehension is predicated upon wider vocabulary, this remains a key element. Aptitudes in visual literacy can help in recognising sight words and those words which don't follow conventions of spelling and so have to be memorised and recognised.

The fluent, comprehending reader

> Even when a reader comprehends the facts of the content, the goal at this stage is deeper: an increased capacity to apply an understanding of the varied uses of words – irony, voice, metaphor and point of view – to go below the surface of the text.

(Wolf, 137, 2008)

At the fluent and comprehending reader stage, readers are increasing their understanding and awareness of the world through encountering and empathising with a range of feelings and varying perspectives, while simultaneously reading to gain knowledge. Reading, at this stage, includes textbooks, reference works, trade books, newspapers and magazines.

The expert reader

> The end of reading development doesn't exist; the unending story of
> reading moves ever forward, leaving the eye, the tongue, the word, the
> author for a new place from which the 'truth breaks forth, fresh, and
> green,' changing the brain and the reader every time.
>
> (Wolf, 162, 2008)

At the expert reader stage, reading occurs across a broad range of
disciplines and written materials.

It is always worth keeping in mind that regardless of reading stage, every
child has the capacity to engage with and enjoy reading. It is important to
create an environment that allows them the freedom to explore their
reading preferences and develop their own love of reading. Award winning
illustrator Shaun Tan (2004) has written about the similarities he sees
between readers of different ages and at different stages:

> Rather than talk about the differences between older and younger readers,
> however, I would prefer to consider what they might actually have in
> common. In particular, we are all interested in playing. We like to look at
> things from unusual angles, attempt to seek some child-like revelation in
> the ordinary, and bring our imagination to the task of questioning everyday
> experience. Why are things the way they are? How might they be different?
> As an artist, these 'childish' activities are the things that preoccupy me
> when I draw pictures and make up stories, and they don't necessitate a
> consideration for any particular audience. What matters are ideas, feelings
> and the pictures and words that build them. How can they be playful and
> subvert our usual expectations? What are the ways that something can be
> represented to most effectively invite us to think and ask questions about
> the world we live in?

Case study 3.1 The Power of Pictures

An understanding of the role visual literacy plays in reading in and of itself
remains a relatively new area. The Centre for Literacy in Primary Education
(CLPE) has developed a training package to support teachers and education
professionals, 'The Power of Pictures.' It grew out of discussions between
Charlotte Hacking and illustrator Ed Vere around the potential that exists for
using picturebooks with older children. When a draft of the new curriculum

was being discussed, Charlotte noticed how little research there was on the subject of visual literacy and moreover relating to the visual arts. Charlotte and Ed were keep to develop a resource to support and empower teachers to feel more confident using visual literacy and illustration in the classroom.

> *'It has surprised me how unfamiliar the children were with looking at pictures in greater depth, really reading what is going on in a picture and being able to explain how they know this.'* (Project teacher, Year 5)

The Power of Pictures is aimed at supporting primary school teachers in developing a better understanding of the craft of picturebook creation and illustration as a means for improving children's reading and writing. Following a two-day training course led by Charlotte and Ed, a range of teaching resources were created free of charge. This includes booklists, teaching plans, key teaching approaches and author and illustrator videos. These resources are available at www.clpe.org.uk/powerofpictures.

Findings from the project showed that picturebooks are an important form of children's books that can aid the development of sophisticated reading skills. Picturebooks can equip readers with the ability to analyse and interpret visuals and to learn about narrative structure, plot and character development in ways that are accessible, engaging and that can support comprehension. Part of these skills included the ability to recognise that words and pictures can convey bias and so enable discussions around navigating visual information literacy.

CLPE also found that children need time, space and planned opportunities for the development of ideas for their creative and independent writing. Alongside the development of reading ability, is an increasing aptitude for creation, using the building blocks children learn to begin constructing their own narratives. The Power of Pictures suggests ways of creative writing that mirror those used by professional writers and illustrators, allowing an authentic experience that moves between the following stages.

Ideation → to creation → reflection → publication

The creative writing opportunities aims to move away from the type of prescribed, factory farming that often occurs in classrooms and which is solely about meeting individual targets. Writing opportunities through the project allows children the opportunity find inspiration on how to construct themes, characters, settings, shapes, structures and patterns. It also enables opportunities for drawing as part of the creative process. Working in this way resulted in extended and independent writing beyond the level that the children had currently been working at.

Feedback from participating teachers revealed a dramatic improvement in their pupils understanding of how stories are structured.

'I had never really considered reading and working with a picturebook at the level I teach (Y5), thinking it would be "too easy" or not engaging enough as a model for writing. How things changed! A small group of children were a little suspicious (they thought it might be "for babies") but in fact they very quickly came around and were amongst the most insightful as the class began to notice the subtle, deeper layers to the text'.
(Project teacher 2013–19)

In the evaluative report on 'The Power of Pictures' former Children's Laureate, author and illustrator Lauren Child commented:

There's not enough understanding of the sophistication of children's books. If we don't understand that, then we don't understand how sophisticated children are and they are amazingly sophisticated and they think very deeply and powerfully about things. And we do them a disservice if we don't see that.

Source: Hacking, Charlotte (2019), The Power of Pictures: Summary of Findings from the Research on the CLPE Power of Pictures Project 2013–19.

A framework for visual competencies

Part of the challenge to our understanding how visual literacy relates to reading development lies in forming a framework for better recognising the skills and competencies which underpin this.

Alongside the phased development of reading, a framework for the analysis of visual literacy is an important means for measuring aptitude and competencies as well as how visual literacy can contribute towards learning and understanding. Callow (2005), categorises the process by which we develop visual literacy into three areas:

- *The affective* – this occurs immediately on viewing an image and is drawn around the sight responses that an individual has.
- *The compositional* – as the name suggests, this draws upon identifying structure and context of what is seen.
- *The critical* – the placement of an image alongside cultural conventions and messaging, thereby moving towards a richer understanding than the immediately literal.

Callow's model has been echoed by Serafini (2014) who suggests the process for interpreting visual texts can be categorised as perceptual, structural and ideological.

It is helpful to draw on existing frameworks in visual literacy teaching to deepen our understanding of how the process of visual literacy operates. Figure 3.2 outlines a series of questions asked in *Visual Literacy in English Language Teaching* (Goldstein, 2016).

Affective or Perceptual	Compositional or Structural	Critical or Ideological
What feelings does the image evoke?	What elements are visible in the foreground and background?	What message does the image transmit?
How does the image evoke these feelings?	Does text accompany the image (titles, captions, explanatory notes)? What does this add to understanding?	How was it created and for what purpose or context?
What other images are brought to mind when viewing it?	How is the image presented or composed?	What media will the image be seen?
Does the image hold any personal relevance, if so what?	What might lie beyond the frame?	Is there an intended audience, what might this reveal about its message?
What does the image remind the viewer of and how?	From what angle or point of view is the image seen?	In what context was the image viewed? The original or another one, what is the difference?
Does the viewer identify with or relate to the image and in what ways?	Which parts of the image are seen first?	Are there different ways the image could be interpreted?
Is the image positive or negative or does it evoke feelings of indifference? Why?	What has been altered, omitted from or included in the image?	Do any of the images conform to stereotypes, idealisation, anachronisms or non-representative constructions?

Figure 3.2 *Questions to support visual literacy as a tool in English Language Teaching*

Together, these questions offer a guided sequence through which the act of looking can be transformed into a series of competencies. The culmination of these aptitudes is a set of critical apparatus, which equips visual readers to better understand and infer meaning from visual information.

Visual literacy in practice

Social and creative opportunities for reading offer engaging ways to populate the stages of reading development with attractive and appealing interventions.

Libraries have seen success using comics as the basis for very popular reading clubs. For example, Cathy Blairs, specialist dyslexia teacher at Beaver Road Primary School in Didsbury runs a reading group that meets every week and is well attended by both girls and boys. The reading group stimulates a great deal of excitement around reading; indeed, the interest of the readers becomes instrumental to the keenness in attending and participating in the group. The reading group have made contact with various comic strip artists who have written to them, answered questions and even sent across original artwork in some instances.

Young people were also encouraged to create their own artwork as part of a scheme for Rochdale Libraries. Rochdale Libraries received a bequest from Annie and Frank Maskew who met in the town library and connected over a shared love of reading and thinking. The money was left to Rochdale to establish collections of literature and philosophy for adults and also for children and young people. The library service at Rochdale also decided to use the money to inaugurate an annual 'Literature and Ideas Festival' as a means of promoting the collection and the themes and subjects it covered. Realising that the festival was not attracting audiences of young people, they worked with magazine producers, Flax, to create a new zine for young people, *Unmasked*. Articles and artwork for the zine was crowd-sourced from young people giving them a sense of ownership over the final product. Photographs and artwork are a key part of the magazine's visual identity and appeal and give an art house vibe to the publication, which is distributed in youth centres, colleges, high schools, libraries and cultural venues across the borough and beyond. The zine website (www.unmaskedzine.com) details the spirit and ethos of *Unmasked*: 'We bring you tales from precarious times. We are not enough and too much. We are unmasked. So venture outside your comfort zone. Read, absorb, engage, pass on.'

It feels apt to end this chapter with a comment from Laurence Anholt (2019) on his personal creative journey and the way the visual experience continues to determine and define his work. The reading journey and the way this influences and shapes our own creative responses, never truly ends during our lifetime.

When I was a small boy, I lived in Holland. One day I was taken to the Vincent van Gogh museum in Amsterdam. I can still remember the excitement – it was like being sucked into a rushing, swirling, multi-coloured snowstorm. The place made me as dizzy as a fairground and from then on, when anyone asked me what I wanted to be, I said '*I want to be an artist.*'

That's why I went to Art School when I was older, and that's why I decided to write and illustrate the 'Anholt's Artists' series. I want everyone to get excited about art, but I also want to tell stories about real people, with real feelings.

These books have helped me to meet so many interesting people – I've visited countless schools around the world, and the story of how I bumped into Sylvette David, Picasso's 'Girl With a Ponytail' would make a book in itself. But what I like most of all are the many letters and emails from readers. Many of them are covered in beautiful drawings – I opened one the other day, which said, '*When I grow up, I want to be an artist.*'

My first job was as an art teacher. I wanted to get my young pupils interested in the great artists, like Vincent van Gogh and Frida Kahlo, who were my heroes. Most artists are outsiders who see the world through different eyes, and I quickly found that the best way to bring these fascinating characters alive was to tell stories and anecdotes about their lives. That's how I came to write and illustrate, *Camille and the Sunflowers*, the first of my 'Anholt's Artists' series, in which the events are seen through the eyes of real children who knew the artists. Thirty-five years later, there are ten books in the series, which are translated into numerous languages and have sold millions of copies in many languages around the world.

In recent years, I have turned my hand to writing full length novels for teens, and currently, adult crime fiction. But for me, it's still a visual experience. In order to make the places and characters believable, I need to see them vividly in my mind's eye. When it's going well, writing fiction is almost like lucid dreaming. You can touch, smell and taste every detail, like a movie in your head. For me, writing is simply painting with words.

Figure 3.3 *Titles featured in 'Anholt's Artists' series* © Laurence Anholt, 2019

CHAPTER 4

Close Inspection: influences and insights into people and processes that shape visual narratives

When effective, the synergy between words and pictures in forming and driving a narrative, can be seamless. Who can think of Julia Donaldson's *The Gruffalo* without also conjuring in their imaginations Axel Scheffler's brilliant illustrations; of Roald Dahl without considering the energetic pen and ink illustrations of Quentin Blake; of Dick Bruna's *Miffy* without visualising his iconic rabbit or Doctor Seuss without bringing to mind the Lorax, or the Grinch? There is an alchemy in how words and pictures cohere to form a consistent narrative. This is achieved through numerous interrelationships, often completely invisible to end-readers and yet as a consequence of these, the finished narrative operates as a cohesive whole.

This chapter examines the various external influencers that shape visual narratives. Economic factors, technology and production all exert influence over what is able to be published and the way in which this happens. This chapter will explore some of the decisions publishers make and the impact this has on readers. An understanding of the ways in which publishing works can help to contextualise how and why certain decisions are made, how this affects the final reading experience and the ways in which libraries, schools, bookshops and educational establishments can collaborate with publishers to create opportunities for reader engagement.

Agents
The journey to publication often begins with an agent. They represent clients, which involves putting them forward for projects, liaising with publishers on their behalf to promote their work and negotiating the best publishing deals. Here we talk with agent Vicki Willden-Lebrecht (2019) who founded The Bright Group International in 2003. The Bright Group is an illustration agency with an international reach, known for its forward thinking approach to the power of illustration.

The Bright Agency is built around our artists and authors, and we believe that the work they do in children's literature is vital for children to grow, explore and learn. Illustration and the ability to create engaging and exciting visual stories are key to a child's learning and literacy. Our artists conjure the weird and wonderful as well as the familiar and relatable onto the page and develop in children a love for books. Allowing kids to explore through visual literacy at a young age will encourage them to become readers for life.

At Bright, everything we do is aimed at supporting our illustrators and authors and celebrating their work. From representation, development and even events in our bookshop-come-gallery, The Bright Emporium, we aim to create a culture that promotes freedom and creativity whilst also sustaining a career in a crowded and competitive market.

Agents play a significant role in finding opportunities for creators to be discovered and eventually published and also in finding opportunities for projects for their existing clients. As Vicki describes, it is important that agents facilitate relationships with authors and publishers that allow their clients freedom and creativity to produce their engaging and exciting visual stories.

Publishers

The role of publishers has been influential in how illustrated books are published and which books get selected for publication. Indeed, some publishers have played a significant role in helping to develop visual narratives as a legitimate form of reading. Klaus Flugge (2019), the founder of Andersen Press has championed quality illustration through his company and its associated relationships for many years. He discusses below the growth of the company from a small publisher to one with international reach that has helped forge international rights fairs:

Andersen Press is now over 40 years old and has become one of the most important publishers of picture books in Great Britain. I started the company with four titles in 1976, two of which were picture books. The discovery of Tony Ross certainly was responsible for the success during the first few years. He is now considered Britain's most popular illustrator. I had published stars like Michael Foreman and Quentin Blake before I started Andersen Press but added quite a number of very talented artists over the next few years, among them Satoshi Kitamura from Japan and Max Velthuijs from Holland. David McKee's first picture book, *Two Can Toucan* started a close cooperation with Andersen and the international success of *Elmer* which is now published in over 70 countries with one new title added every year, apart from board books and novelty books. But lots of new and young talent has been added every year. I was given the Eleanor Farjeon Award some years ago for my contribution to children's books and the Freedom of the City of Bologna for helping to establish what is now the most important children's book fair in the word. Andersen has been very successful in selling foreign rights of its books, a very essential part in publishing quality full colour picture books and the list continues to grow thanks to it and also the many discerning librarians supporting children's books.

Economically, the picturebook market is a challenging one. In the UK, picturebooks often require co-editions in order that their publication is financially viable. This means a book is sold to another country or territory, for simultaneous (or near-simultaneous) publication. This enables savings to be made through economy of scale on printing. Selling foreign rights has also become increasingly important to the children's book market. After 25 years working at Andersen Press, Sarah Peckenham established the picturebook publishing house, Scallywag Press. Sarah explains that after spending so long selling the rights for books that others had bought, she wanted to have a go at publishing the books herself.

Sarah discusses the two models for publication that they use at Scallywag Press. One is buying co-rights for publications from overseas like those by illustrator Jon Agee. The UK and commonwealth rights are bought in, which gives a smaller overall market potential but carries less risk and they are able to publish quickly as the product is already developed. The second model that can make for a higher investment is to bring in editors and designers and produce a totally new title to take to the market with the potential to cover costs and make profits through selling the rights to co-editions. Sarah describes it as being useful for Scallywag to employ a mix of both models.

In terms of discovering new talent to create the Scallywag Press list, Sarah describes how important she has found the MA courses. Illustrator and fine artist Jonathan Farr introduced her to a student on the

Cambridge illustration course: Rose Robbins, author and illustrator of *Me and My Sister* and from the same MA course Sarah has bought *Umbrella*, a picturebook by Elena Arevalo Melville.

As shown above, there are a number of different ways that publishers will interact with the marketplace in their search for talent. With the advent of pictorial social media platforms like Instagram, this is becoming an increasingly valuable way for aspiring illustrators to showcase their work and style and for publishers to discover new talent.

Graphic design and print

The role of design is key in terms of how readers encounter illustrated works. Designers can be in-house or freelance who are commissioned according to a brief. When we talk about design of picturebooks, we are referring to the size, shape, layout, typography and even the choice of paper it is printed on. Design and print decisions are vital to the overall look and feel of an illustrated work and will certainly influence how the illustrations are experienced by the reader. Ziggy Hanaor (2019) from Cicada Books discusses how design can enrich the reading experience:

> I come from an art and design book background, so the presentation of the book is very important to me. The layout of the pages and the production effects can turn a book into something that you want to touch and hold, and that's the Holy Grail. I work very closely with a design studio called Studio April. We talk a lot about what kind of paper to print on, and what production effects to use. Pantone printing, use of a neon, or a foil or embossing on the cover, can really make a difference to the shelf appeal of a book. However, price point is also key, so there's always a balance that needs to be struck.
>
> I work with a handful of printers who I trust and, touch wood, I haven't had too many dreadful disasters. I have blank dummies made, and I check the paper quality before printing. On a book where we're using pantones, I'll get a wet proof, but this is super expensive, so if it's a straightforward book I might not.

Design choices will include how the text sits upon the page and where this is located in relation to illustrations. A key part of the synergy between the two is ensuring both are sited appropriately so as to inter-relate. In picturebooks this will often include ensuring page-turns happen at the appropriate juncture creating drama or humour. It may also include the use of special elements like die-cuts or lamination to help bring the story to life. Designers will often consult with sales and marketing teams in creating a cover that will support selling the book across its key markets and accounts.

Anna Lubecka runs Banana Bear Books, and is a children's focused graphic designer who studied illustration, fine art, photography and graphic design at the University of the Arts in London. Anna describes her role:

> I'm a children's book Art Director and Designer. My passion is for picturebooks. I love working closely with authors and illustrators, putting their words and illustrations together to tell a visually exciting story, bursting with page turners, humour and emotion. I also like coming up with ideas for exciting new novelty formats, from die cuts to pop-up surprises. Whether it's art directing new characters or creating fun layouts, my passion is to bring everything together into a beautiful book or gift package for children to enjoy and treasure.

The relationship between words and pictures is paramount in creating a book that children will enjoy and treasure as Anna describes. Freelance designer, Zoe Tucker, provides an insight into picturebooks and design: what's important and why.

Picturebooks and design: what's important and why

Design: We spend a lot of time faffing with fonts, picking exactly the right one, and crafting it across the page! A picture book is approximately 700 words, and people are sometimes surprised to hear that I will often design each and every word so it sits comfortably alongside the artwork. Where possible we try to break up big blocks of text, and sit smaller blocks, single sentences or even single words in and around the artwork. We work closely with the artist to ensure there is enough space for the text, in all the right places. (We also have to allow a little more space for foreign editions. A German translation of an English text, for instance, can run at least a third longer!)

Easy reading: A good picture book incorporates a nice clear easy reading font, something that is legible and accessible. We try to imagine a parent reading the book at bedtime and make sure that the font choice and size are clear in dimmed lighting.

Pacing: When we're designing and developing the book with the editor, artist and author, we spend a lot of time talking about pacing. This is the overall rise and fall of the story, which brings the drama – the highs and lows. As part of the conversation, we consider the page breaks and most importantly how someone will read the book aloud. Where they will naturally pause, or get animated. (We always make a mock-up of the book and read it aloud to each other – it's really helpful!) The designer can manipulate this further with the design and layout of the text on the page. We try to give visual clues to the parent/reader to help them get the most enjoyment from reading the book.

Strong characters: The designer and illustrator take a lot of time over characterisation and the best books, by the best artists, should effortlessly demonstrate this. There is a reason Axel Sheffler's books are popular – his characters have lots of warmth and humour. The subtle expressions shared between two characters can bring a story to life. Good picture books extend this through not just the main character, but into the background characters too, providing secondary storylines for children to spot in the pictures. The designer and editor work closely with the illustrator to help develop these additional narratives. It's fun and gives the illustrator a chance to put their own stamp on things. Did you know Axel has hidden a little Gruffalo in every picture book he has illustrated since he did the original Gruffalo?

A good cover: What makes a good cover? This is subject to so much discussion, and one thing that is true – we all judge a book by its cover! The designer usually gets a feel for the cover design during the early stages of the project, particularly once the artist has made all the roughs for the interior pages. I find there is usually one or two images that jump out and provide an imme-diate starting point. The main aim is to catch the eye, draw the reader in with strong character and to also give a little bit of storytelling – something that conveys the mood and content of the book. Cover design is subjective, and goes through a lengthy process to get it right. We take into account where the book will be seen, who it's aimed at, what age is the reader, who is buying the book (parent, carer, grandparent, child) and finally who is the compe-tition. All these factors (and no doubt more that I've forgotten) play a part in how we design the cover. Is the character the main focus, or perhaps the title lettering? What is the cover finish, do we want to use any special finishes (foil, die-cut, glitter, flocking etc.). For picturebooks we are often appealing to the guardian as well as the child (the person who is buying the book, or picking up the book is the guardian). For middlegrade fiction and above we are appealing to the child, by that age they are picking and choosing their own books. They are like magpies at this age and drawn to anything bright and shiny!

Harmony in words and pictures

Sometimes a picturebook is created by one person who has both written and illustrated the work; often, however, picturebooks are the coming together of an author and illustrator whose forms must work together to create synergy between words and pictures. There is no standard way for how the collaboration between author and illustrator works, in some instances the creators may have an existing relationship or they may have come up with the picturebook concept together, on other occasions a relationship might be brokered by publishers. Ziggy Hanaor (2019) comments on this process:

> Some books start with a story and some books start with an illustrator. Books that start with a story are easier. If I have a strong story, I can usually visualise the way it needs to look. I'm all over Instagram and the blogs, so then it's a matter of finding the right illustration style. The books that start with an illustrator are a bit more complex. If I find an illustrator whose work I love, I'll meet with them and we'll try to find a subject that engages them. I then work with a couple of writers to develop the idea into something more concrete. Sometimes that's easy and sometimes it really is not.
>
> Occasionally, I get pitched a book that's in a really good state. Henry Blackshaw pitched me *Inner Child*, and as soon as I saw it, I thought – YES! There have been another couple recently that prompted the same reaction, but this is definitely a new development.

David Fickling, founder of David Fickling Books and the editor who paired author Jacqueline Wilson with illustrator Nick Sharratt and author Terry Deary with illustrator Martin Brown commented on the art of making these pairings: 'to start, the relationship ship has to be mediated. It is the job of the editor to make sure this works and to maintain the quality. They start the fire but it is the reading experience which decides its success.'

In an interview in *ACHUKA*, author and illustrator, Chris Mould (2007), provided insight into the process of working in collaboration with authors to illustrate their work:

> Some writers are very visual and others aren't at all which I find intriguing. It often brings out differences between authors and illustrators but I really feel that if you go down the creative line together instead of alone it will

result in something better. Paul Stewart and Chris Riddell have an excellent working relationship that means that their books evolve out of the time they spend together in creative thought. I think that's brilliant. Ian Ogilvy is a very visually minded writer. We often go through a process where he says, 'I didn't really see this character like that, I saw him/her like this.' I like this because I can't think of a situation where the idea of pushing the drawing around hasn't worked. I like to get everybody in on things. It works for me but for some illustrators it doesn't and I understand the frustration because people have to work in the way that is best for them.

In the same interview, author and illustrator Nick Ward (2007) added his thoughts on the process of illustrating the work of other writers:

I think you have to be honest to yourself and the author. You must try and illustrate a book the way you want to do it, but remain true to the author's vision. An illustrator must be in harmony with a story, otherwise it can become soulless – and this does happen! I suppose the most frustrating thing is to be chosen to illustrate a book, and then be asked to draw in the style of someone else. It rarely works!

Roald Dahl Funny Prize award-winning author, Peter Bently (2019), discusses the relationship between written language and illustrations, giving his perspective as an author and further describing how words and pictures can interrelate to create moments of humour:

I often say that when I write a picture book text I am actually writing *half* a story. The other half is the job of the illustrator, and I have been incredibly fortunate to work with some superb ones. For me what marks out the most outstanding illustrators is their ability not simply to draw exactly, and only, what the story says – or what I myself might suggest in any notes – but also literally to 'add lustre' by including extra little visual elements of their own. A lot of my picture books are humorous and a good illustrator can enrich the comedy by providing little side narratives and subplots alongside the main 'action'. For example, in his wonderful illustrations to *The Prince and the Porker* (Andersen Press), David Roberts includes the tiny figure of a mouse who follows the main character from scene to scene, variously peeping out of a palace chamber pot, skittering upstairs or mischievously running off with a dropped humbug. It adds an extra layer of humour and richness – and I have found that once they spot the mouse, children love looking for it on every spread. If you get commissioned to work with an illustrator of such quality more than once, you can get wise to this, for example by consciously not overloading the story with text in order to allow the artist full rein to their talent.

To achieve the 'harmony' Nick describes and which Peter alludes to, an awareness of the synergy between words and pictures is important, both in appraising visual stories and when creating these. Multi-award-winning author, Nicola Davies, provides some top tips on how to achieve this. These are useful both for creators, but also in appraising how the relationship between words and pictures is operating.

Top tips for achieving good synergy between words and pictures

Tip 1: The first tip may sound obvious, but publishers don't always get it right, and it is 'choose the right partners'! Every text has its own atmosphere and voice and that will only really be complemented by a particular illustrative style. These writer/artist marriages are crucial to the success of a picture book. Marriages of convenience where a publisher is looking for a vehicle for a favoured artist sometimes work, but not always.

Tip 2: Dialogue. Writer and artist need to talk at some point in the process. The best results happen when this conversation comes early on, even perhaps before the text is written, so the story develops as the two voices of words and pictures counterpoint each other. This is a very individual process and sometimes the dialogue happens on its own, without writer and artist even meeting.

Tip 3: Good design. The role of the art director/designer in the creation of picture books is largely overlooked, but is VITAL. Good designers work with artists to make the best use of their work – perhaps reducing or enlarging art work to make more impact on the page. Then there's the art of placing the text, choosing the font and deciding which words go on which page. Page turns are the scene changers of picture books and pagination – the process of deciding where they come is largely the realm of the designer. Great words and great pictures that match beautifully can be let down by poor design.

Tip 4: Teamwork. Picture books take good editors, good designers as well as good artists and writers to create. This teamwork and team dialogue should continue right the way through the process and include a final review stage where no one should be afraid to suggest radical changes.

Tip 5: KNOW WHEN TO STOP. It is entirely possible with a picture book text and with its relationship with pictures to go round and round in editorial circles, waste time and end up with something worse than what you started with. Part of this tip is BE BRAVE...If you've done something strange, original, weird or dark don't be afraid of it. Kids are more emotionally sophisticated than you think and with words and pictures working together, they can understand nuanced messages and cope with darkness. Remember at all times that the picture book is a powerful and unique art form, and although ignored and even reviled by the cultural elite it is a hugely important form, with the ability to speak across ages and cultures in a way that only music can equal.

Representation and translation

Visual images can transcend language and therefore, play an important role as a means of communicating and aiding understanding of other cultures and experiences. With this comes significant responsibility to ensure that what is being represented is done so in a way that is respectful to these cultures. The power of illustration to convey information and traditions from other countries and cultures should not be under-estimated. It is important that publishers work with diverse creators that contribute to the creation of authentic cultural experiences and characters. One way publishers may diversify their list is by importing titles into the market place through translation.

Alice Curry (2019) – founder of Lantana Publishing the award-winning inclusive publishing house, and former winner of the Kim Scott Walwyn Prize for women in publishing – discusses how she and her company seek to increase representation in children's illustration:

> As commissioning editor for Lantana, I am keen to offer our readers the chance to explore a wealth of cultural styles yet am aware of how difficult it can be to discover and nurture diverse talent. Where current mechanisms for discovery often tend to overlook illustrators with non-traditional profiles or non-linear paths into publishing (those who may not – for instance – have chosen, or been able, to undertake an arts degree or equivalent), Lantana has taken a proactive approach to commissioning. This includes looking to other industries for untapped talent (obvious places are advertising, greetings cards, animation); expanding the search beyond UK borders (several of Lantana's illustrators have won international awards in countries

such as Russia, Poland, Syria, Argentina, Brazil and Japan); mentoring un-agented and un-published illustrators (found via portfolios at book fairs, the slush pile). One of our greatest successes – and one of my personal highlights – has been facilitating the meteoric rise of Poonam Mistry, who's debut picturebook *You're Safe With Me* went on to be shortlisted for the Kate Greenaway Medal 2019, and whose combination of British education and Indian arts heritage gives her a unique hybridised style that brings something truly new to the publishing landscape.

Greet Pauwelijn (2019), founder of independent publisher Book Island who publishes picturebooks from around the world, talks about translation and the importance of funding in making this financially viable in the UK marketplace:

> We translate and publish beautifully-illustrated and thought-provoking picture books from around the globe. In the world's current climate, translated picture books are more important than ever because they help to foster empathy and understanding of other cultures. Our latest title, *Mum's Jumper*, is about a little girl struggling with coming to terms with the death of her mother and we hope to see it used by many schools and libraries as a way to explore grief with children in an honest and accessible way.
>
> Thanks to generous EU funding, next year we will be publishing two picture books that discuss other cultures, one set in Sweden and during the revolution in Iran. These offer children an insight into the lives of other children across different countries and different times.

A real sense of affirmation occurs when children identify with characters in books that are from similar backgrounds, lifestyles or cultures to them. To facilitate this sense of belonging, it is so important for the publishing industry to produce books that every child can see themselves repre-sented in. There is an increasing understanding that visual representation is vital to children seeing themselves reflected in books; not only do we want young people to be able to use their imaginations to visualise themselves as the characters they read, we want them to see themselves, their friends, and their families reflected in the illustrations they see. Importing books in translation is one way to include more diverse stories and experiences but it is also essential that due care is given to acquiring creators from a diverse range of backgrounds (see Chapter 5 for further discussion on the importance of visual representation).

Case study 4.1   Imagination to implementation: creating *The Lost Words*

In exploring the various roles that are carried out by publishers, it is useful to see this in action by tracking the production of a book and the processes that it undergoes. This case study, focuses on *The Lost Words* written by Robert MacFarlane and illustrated by Jackie Morris. The book has captured the public attention in extraordinary ways including a dedicated exhibition held at Compton Verney, crowd-funding initiatives to gift copies of the book to every primary school in Scotland and an ever-growing number of additional areas of the United Kingdom, readers going on their own nature pilgrimages; it has even inspired folk-song interpretations and formed the basis for a cross-arts concert at the 2019 Proms. In addition to these accolades, *The Lost Words* became the winner of the CILIP Kate Greenaway Medal for outstanding illustration in 2019.

The idea for the book itself grew out of a conversation between illustrator Jackie Morris and then children's books editor of *The Guardian*, Emily Drabble. Recognising the value of the natural world in children's lives, a range of authors, naturalists and broadcasters signed a letter requesting that the Oxford Junior English dictionary reinstate twenty words all relating to the natural world that had been removed from the dictionary. Among those who signed the letter were Margaret Atwood, Nicola Davies, Robert MacFarlane, Michael Morpurgo, Sir Andrew Motion and Jackie Morris. Describing the decision Jackie states, 'it highlighted the disconnect between language and nature and was a clear indication that something was wrong.'

Jackie and Emily discussed creating a web slideshow of images to highlight the words that had been dropped. Fearing that a slideshow would be ephemeral and not have the length of use, Jackie began to think about a book. She wrote to co-signatory, Robert MacFarlane who had written *The Old Ways* (a book about traditions rooted in landscape and lore), asking if he might consider penning an introduction. He responded in a couple of weeks suggesting there was an opportunity for a more in depth collaboration than writing an introduction.

Jackie and Robert began to explore ideas between them. Jackie was clear that she did not want children to be directly in the book and that she wanted it to be wild. Jackie recalled 'For Robert the idea of spells clicked in his mind. The first one he wrote was the kingfisher and I painted it against a background of gold-leaf.' Here Jessica Woollard, Robert's agent and latterly

Jackie's agent discusses the role of the agent as a 'facilitator' and how she was inspired by the collaboration between writer and artist:

> As agents we are facilitators, working on the one hand to develop a creative project and help it to achieve its maximum potential and on the other hand to vouchsafe and protect it both legally and as a creative entity. With an illustrated work, there is the interplay between words and images, sometimes written by different people so requiring co-ordination. With *The Lost Words*, the interplay between Jackie and Robert was in fact the beginning of a great creative friendship, which then blossomed into a cultural phenomenon. There is an online map showing which areas of the UK have the book crowd funded into every primary school. The book is powerfully speaking to and being used around the end of life, as well as young children/the start of life. Campaigns which placed the book in every care home in Wales are now extending to the whole of Britain, also for hospices, GP surgeries and the art and spells are covering three floors of a new London hospital. The Spell Songs project united some of the most famous names in the European folk scene, a stunning performance at the Southbank Centre and the accompanying album is into its second tour. Lots of musical adaptations, from The Boston Symphony Orchestra and its children's choir, a Prom, exhibitions of the artwork, nature walks in National Trust properties. I could go on. As the book spawned a movement and broke out of its boundaries into so many other areas, so we all grew and developed with it.
>
> Jackie and Robert brought a wealth of experience and dedication to the creation of *The Lost Words*, that is what gives it such a solid grounding, combined with Robert's brilliance with language and Jackie's talent as an artist and her understanding of how people respond to space as well as image on the page, all went towards making this such a special and unusual book.

Robert contacted his publisher, Simon Prosser at Hamish Hamilton, who was interested in the idea of the collaboration. Robert, Jackie and Jessica were then invited into a meeting with Hamish Hamilton's editorial team, a production team and members of the publicity and marketing teams. Robert and Jackie spoke about their vision for the book and how it could be published. Hamish Hamilton had not done anything that wasn't exclusively for adults and nothing that was illustrated so it was a bold venture for them into uncharted territory.

Presenting the book at the Hamish Hamilton offices, was the first time Jackie and Robert met and they would not do so again until the project had been completed. The initial kingfisher spell created by Robert and painted by Jackie enabled discussions around how the form could work, what needed to be considered in terms of production and scale and how the collaboration might happen. The two-hour meeting was a productive one and all participants left feeling energised and inspired.

The publisher, Simon, then presented the idea internally to the team and acquired the book in the standard way. It was then scheduled in advance so that there would be time to produce the work and to research production and printing.

Jackie and Robert were physically apart for most of the creative process, communicating and sharing their work via emails. Jackie explained, 'everything was done via email, I'd send sketches, he would send spells to be spoken aloud. It was the most collaborative piece of work of all of the things I've done.'

Robert discusses his experience of the collaboration:

Spells have always been written to be spoken, as it were; utterance is the source of their magic and power. So I knew from early on that I wanted to write in a way that encouraged – even required – reading aloud. Jackie was always the first to see a spell once I'd drafted it, and I would send it to her with the cover message: 'To be read aloud.' Jackie also gave me permission, so to speak, to compose the spells using the fully mustered force of language as I knew it; to weave sound patterns, embed dozens of part-rhymes, and to include words – such as 'susurrus', in the Adder Spell, or 'furze' in the Wren Spell – that might not be recognisable in terms of meaning to children, but that would taste good in the mouth, sound rich and strange in the ear; and might, just might, send them off to the dictionary or the internet to discover a meaning. And, of course, many of these more difficult or arcane words were given life and sense by Jackie's art.

Jackie began sending photographs of what she was painting to the publisher and later started to send the physical artwork which was scanned in at high resolution for use in the book.

Designer Alison O'Toole who was the in-house designer at Hamish Hamilton for *The Lost Words* was assigned the project and came back with an early treatment. From early on it was recognised there was a need to decide on the design template and overall aesthetic. The three-fold triptych structure was chosen as this would visually evoke the idea of visibility, absence and disappearance of the 'lost' word and these three spreads would recur throughout the book. A few different routes for evoking absence were explored but the decision was made to have a scattering of letters on the absence pages, echoing the iconography.

The template was set before most of the artwork and text was received, providing a framework that Robert and Jackie, together with the production team, were working towards. There followed a 9 to 12 month schedule where Robert and Jackie would deliver their work in tranches with sets of the artwork and text for the spells.

The artwork was sent to the reproduction house, a separate company, where they were scanned and photographed. Experimentation was had to determine the best method for reproducing the different types of goldleaf used by Jackie in her artwork, each of which had different qualities and levels of shimmer. Metallic pantones were tested but these returned a flat reproduction, only producing one shade and not allowing the variation of colour and light to come through. Different variations and types of paperstock and ink were tested until Jackie and Robert agreed on the final production specifications.

A decision also had to be reached about the reproduction of Jackie's paintings, there was some question about whether to have full bleeds, or to show the physical edge of the paintings themselves, giving an idea of their construction. Jackie felt it was important these did not have messy edges and full bleeds were agreed.

Once complete, the paintings and spells were sent to the designer, Alison, who composed the page layouts and each composition was sent back to Robert and Jackie to approve. Alison and Jackie were conscious that they wanted the book to be interactive and for readers to engage with it while also ensuring it was beautiful and appeared as a work of art as opposed to having the feel of an activity book. . The finished book achieved both interactivity and beauty; creating a captivating experience where readers could engage, finding letters, tracing words out while enjoying the richness of the artwork, particularly in the final pages as the eyes are drawn to different parts. The larger size of the book was selected so that the book could be *stepped into* creating an immersive reading experience.

Following an editing and proofreading process, a cover was produced using one of Jackie's paintings from inside the book. Before arriving at this cover, however, there were a number of iterations, with an in-house design initially proposed. The team agreed on a full cover illustration with Jackie suggesting a stripped back aesthetic as all felt it was important to convey a sense of movement and life in the image but that it needed to feel clean, confident and lacking in busyness. Alongside the designer and editorial team, the sales and communications teams were involved in the cover design process.

As a by-product of using goldleaf in Jackie's paintings, the residual outlines of the square sheets were left on the page creating silhouetted style images, almost like imprints of the image being created of the kingfisher, otter and so on. Jackie was keen that these silhouettes were used as icons; they aligned neatly with the idea of presence and absence so fitted the theme of the book well. These silhouettes were also used as endpapers and were often requested in press releases, becoming a part of the visual language of the book carrying the visual idea of being the ghost of an image, or an echo.

Descriptive copy was created – which Robert was involved with – and consideration was then given to positioning the title in the market and the campaign around it. It was agreed that the importance of language and concepts of the natural world were central to this but also that the book should be for all ages and not pigeon-holed as one that only children would enjoy given that Robert and Jackie had both approached creating the written and pictorial text in a way that was not dumbed down or condescending. It was also felt that there could be a campaigning strand to the book since it carried an important message about the natural world.

Responses to the book have been phenomenal including an incredible amount of supporting educational resources that have been created. As part of the CILIP Kate Greenaway shortlisting, resources were created to enable interaction with the book by shadowing groups and reading groups across the United Kingdom who took part in the scheme. Amy McKay from Corby Business Academy and Co-ordinator for the CILIP Carnegie and Kate Greenaway Awards discusses ways of sharing *The Lost Words:* 'the large format itself helps it feel like an incredibly special book and one that creates a sense of awe when starting to share it. It is almost like a tactile book, people want to reach out to stroke it and trace out words almost as an involuntary reaction.' In creating activities for students to engage with, Amy worked upon *Where's Wally* style searches where readers were encouraged to hunt for different visual elements. For older readers they worked on art appreciation and used the pictures as a springboard to find out more about the natural world, to discover personal connections and explore the environment around them. Amy organised conker fights to tie in with the pages featuring this and the groups undertook their own illustrations hiding words and challenging one another to find what they had hidden in their own pictures.

Numerous events have been held at venues and festivals across the length and breadth of the country, and a key part of these have included Jackie live painting, capturing the minds and imagination of her audience as she recites the spells as incantations, whilst painting otters and foxes. Hermione Thompson (2019), part of the editorial team at Hamish Hamilton, commented: 'Jackie's live painting gives an invitation to look behind the curtain and to empower people to get involved themselves giving the idea that art can be much more open and collaborative.'

Rights for *The Lost Words* have been bought in different territories and the book has been published in other languages. Poet Mererid Hopwood (2019) discusses translating the book for its Welsh edition:

> Saving words and languages matters. It matters because they are more than just sounds. They are windows that enable us to see and understand the world about us. A bluebell and a dandelion may both be flowers, but without being called by their own names, they become somehow less visible, less important, more prone to be ignored ... and eventually, more likely to vanish.
>
> This is one of the reasons why I was so delighted to be asked to try to recast Robert Macfarlane's *spells* into Welsh and project them against Jackie Morris' extraordinarily beautiful artwork. Inspired by the original ideas, I took a deep breath and imagined my pencil into a magic wand. Together we were facing a task of great responsibility – to conjure the words of the world about us back from the brink of unbeing and place them in central sight!

When the book won the CILIP Kate Greenaway Medal for illustration, it was testament to the craftsmanship and thought present in Jackie's work, the synergy that exists with Robert's words and the careful design and collaborative approach throughout every stage of publication. Discussing the reasons for the book winning the CILIP Kate Greenaway Medal in *The Bookseller* (Eyre, 2019a), Chair of the 2019 judging panel, Alison Brumwell stated:

> The illustrations test our acuity and make us all think on a much deeper level about scale, colour and proportion; also, about representations of loss and absence. We are invited to 'read' on more than one level and to reflect upon a world in which change can mean irreparable loss, impoverishing both language and the environment. This is an astonishing book, which deserves the highest accolades.

Figure 4.1 *Illustrator Jackie Morris pictured with the Kate Greenaway Medal and her winning book The Lost Words,* photo courtesy of Katariina Jarvinen, © CILIP 2019

Pictures Mean Business

Illustration has sometimes been the poor relation in publishing and the book trade. Pictures Mean Business is a movement that author and illustrator Sarah McIntyre has created to try to highlight the benefits of crediting illustrators for their work and recognising the value this brings to all areas of the book trade. The movement recognises that illustrators need to have visibility not just through the work, but also to be properly accredited in order to have a successful, ongoing career.

Using the hashtag #PicturesMeanBusiness to draw focus and attention to the role of illustration in children's books, the movement has helped change attitudes and inequalities in the sector. An example of this has been with the CILIP Kate Greenaway and Carnegie Medals. Whereas the Kate Greenaway Medal for illustration has always credited the authors of the books that are in contention, the Carnegie Medal had not previously reciprocated through recognising the illustrators of books. Sarah pointed this out to the Awards working party and the decision was made to ensure that authors and illustrators for both Medals would be referenced in all materials created by the awards. The Pictures Mean Business initiative seeks to ensure that all involved with books recognise the role of illustration and the ways this can help support and build readers of the future.

In the case study that follows Sarah McIntyre discusses the initiative and contemplates why embedding illustration and the people who create these is crucial not just for the career of illustrators themselves but for individuals as creators too.

Case study 4.2   Pictures Mean Business

Teaching children to credit the people who make things is a vital part of them learning how to make things themselves. There's a reason celebrity chefs inspire people to cook or bake: food doesn't just magically appear, viewers and readers realise there's a person who makes these things, that it involves a process, and they see that the process is something they could do themselves. Children don't immediately grasp the concept that books are created by real people. Teachers frequently mention writers such as Roald Dahl and JK Rowling to inspire children's writing. But mentioning illustrators can be just as inspiring for children's creativity, sometimes even more so, because children connect with pictures before they connect with written words. I find that if I put a blank sheet of paper in front of a child and ask them to 'write a story', they often freeze up. But if I lead them through drawing a character, their excitement bubbles over and they are full of ideas about where that character lives, what it likes, what it might do, all wonderful ingredients for telling a story.

Pictures matter. The people who make pictures matter, too, whether they be the professionals who create lavish illustrations, or a child who's drawing a three-headed monster for the first time. Paying close attention to children talking with you about a picture they've just created fills them with a sense of pride in their work, and opens up a warm channel of communication. Showing them pictures in books created by other people, and talking about the pictures gives them fresh ideas for what they can draw, talk about and write about. Attempts to wean children off pictures can be harmful; this teaches them that things they love about books aren't acceptable, and may tarnish their love of reading overall. And it's hypocritical; adults who want children to read books without pictures may spend their own free time scrolling through photos and cartoons on social media, and flicking through glossy magazines.

The people who create these pictures – illustrators – don't live off of fairy dust and wishes, they need to make a living in the same way writers do. If we want our children to encounter the best illustration possible, we need to support illustrators by helping them build names for themselves in the profession. Everyone knows the name Quentin Blake, but how many other illustrators can they list? If we can make our best illustrators household names, in the same way we do with David Walliams, these illustrators will get a tremendous career boost in an industry where it's surprisingly hard to survive. And it teaches respect: you wouldn't applaud a child for stealing another child's toy and passing it off as their own. But when people come up with an inspirational quote to put on the internet, often they will happily grab a piece of artwork and post it as though they created it themselves. This sharing of uncredited art does nothing to boost that illustrator's career. In the same way, many writers will post brand-new cover artwork and receive its praise as though they created that artwork themselves, denying an illustrator a possibly career-defining moment that would have given them far more illustration work, and possibly invitations to teach or do paid events. Crediting artwork teaches children that they can't just take things, they need to respect the people who made them, and at the same time opens up joyous opportunities for them to discover a whole new world of art, creativity and story.

Pictures Mean Business offers a model and guidelines to better value illustration and the creative processes and people behind these to help create a more robust and sustainable business. Suggestions on the Pictures Mean Business website include:

- Creating displays that use the visual identity of a book by using its illustrator and properly attributing these can create an engaging way to promote books.
- Using book covers on social media can be a powerful way to create traction and engagement around particular titles, copying in illustrators as well as authors, recognises their creative work and increases potential reach.
- When creating interviews or information on authors, make sure to include details about the illustrators who have been involved too.
- When reviewing illustrated titles, make sure to mention the pictures and the impact or response they cause as well as talking about the writing, be sure to credit both authors and illustrators.
- If running sessions on particular books reference artists and explore the illustrations and their relationship with the writing.

As well as providing best practice guidance, suggestions are also given on the website for activities:

- Gaining understanding of the way visual storytelling happens in sequence by creating a story scroll using a roll of paper with children drawing upon this in sequence.
- Exploring elements in the story that are not mentioned in the writing but can be seen in the pictures.
- Thinking about how mood is set in the book; considering the colour palette and colour changes might be useful in this.
- Illustrators often work using very different styles and media, children can be encouraged to draw animals or a self-portrait in the style of one of the illustrators.
- Reinterpret texts, read a picturebook to children but stop at key moments in the story encouraging them to draw the way the page might look. Try exploring fairytale retellings with works like Jon Scieszka and illustrator Lane Smith's *The True Story of the Three Little Pigs* or Mini Grey's *The Pea and the Princess*.
- Create story murals using art and Illustration throughout the school to help inspire creativity, stories and to celebrate illustrators.

Find out more at www.picturesmeanbusiness.com.

A comic perspective

Comic books have played an important role in British popular culture, with the late 1930s to 1950s considered the golden age of comics. As picture-based stories, comics are highly accessible in their form and came to be seen as childish with children becoming the primary market, or as having low cultural value. Comics have, nonetheless, played a huge role in popular culture influencing film, media and the arts with works like those of pop-artist Roy Lichtenstein.

Unfortunately, despite being massively enjoyed by young people, the comic book form was side-lined from education and became stigmatised. This decline in the comic book industry can be traced back to the 1970s; speaking with publisher David Fickling (2019), an avid reader of comics as a child, he describes how it is often stated that the decline of comics was largely due to television, but he believes it was firmly tied to business reasons too. He explains that comics, which largely followed the newspaper model of production, were facing the same fate as daily newspapers as people's approach to retrieving information was changing.

Comics had commonly been printed in huge numbers, *The Eagle* founded by a vicar from Preston, Marcus Morris, sold 900,000 copies of its first issue and soon secured a weekly circulation of almost a million copies. The business model for comics, however, was broken and alongside the cultural stigma, David explains there was a lack of value or worth attributed to comic book illustrators which often resulted in underpayment and lack of attribution. Some years later, these factors helped to inform the creation of *David Fickling Comics* in 2008 and its successor *The Phoenix* as David describes, he wanted to create a business model where makers were paid properly and create comics that would create excitement and engagement in reading.

The types of visual patterning in comics can aid children with dyslexia for whom blocks of text can be overwhelming. The key to good comic storytelling David says is the sense of story itself. Devising the *David Fickling Comics* was a means for engaging experienced illustrators and authors from the children's book world in creating a comic that children could know was specifically for them and that was purely for the pleasure of storytelling. David was clear he wanted the comic to be published on a weekly basis, feeling that this was the optimum time for children to read its content and not to have to wait too long before the next issue was ready for them.

One of the challenges in establishing *David Fickling Comics* was persuading people that children would want to read comics, when there were so few active children's comics publishing. Random House were persuaded to try producing comics on the basis that David formulated a successful economic model that they could replicate. In 2008, the *David Fickling Comic* released the first new weekly comic published in the UK for over 20 years. Although small, the company is flourishing and is based on talent, teamwork and a commitment to publish the very best stories.

Mike Stirling (2019), Editorial Director and Head of Beano Studios Scotland further provides insight into the role that comics can play in children's reading:

> *Beano* has successfully developed a love of reading across generations of children. It's been a tried and tested way to establish a weekly reading habit in children for over 81 years, and almost 30 million people alive in the UK today have been a regular visitor to Beanotown at some – typically golden – point in their lives. Since the launch of Beano.com in 2016, the weekly comic has bucked a downward publishing trend an instead increased sales over 10% year on year.

Parents, guardians and teachers know that they can trust *Beano* to engage even reluctant readers because our comic strips use fewer words than a typical storybook and scaffold the experience with pictures. That's because we create based upon a rule that every story must be understandable, first and foremost, via the pictures alone.

Not only does this guarantee wide enfranchisement, but also leaves us space to develop additional ideas and themes via the words, rewarding a deeper engagement even further. Every issue guarantees fresh vocabulary, perfectly pitched humour and entertaining storylines.

Comics can subtly overcome negative perceptions of reading. The pure entertainment they engender encourages kids to overlook any effort involved, because they're actually enjoying the process.

The process of reading a comic is far from passive. There are gaps in the action that each panel serves up, necessitating that the reader must fill these from their own imagination. The structure serves up a sort of visual script that the reader acts out.

This leads to greater confidence and encourages deeper time investment, confirmed by the fact *Beano* readers enjoy reading at the rate of more than a chapter book per month. That's on top of 144 pages of comic strip!

It's widely recognised that improved literacy skills can open more doors to learning for years to come, suggesting *Beano* is the 'missing link' that everyone who cares about maximising children's life opportunities should be aware of. We were really proud to partner with the Summer Reading Challenge in 2018 – the first time a comic was used as the theme.

Librarians tell us they enjoy using *Beano* as a stimulus because they intrinsically understand the characters, having already become friends with them during their own childhood. This equals a great shared-experience talking point. The fact our characters are often featured enjoying reading in the comic also allows them to be used to start positive conversations about reading being fun.

As Mike mentioned, in 2018 The Reading Agency's popular 'Summer Reading Challenge' focused on *Beano* characters and was titled 'Mischief Makers'. This was to help celebrate the 80th anniversary of *The Beano* comic. The scheme encourages children to visit libraries and read six books across the lengthy summer holidays as a means for maintaining literacy levels, continuing and developing reading for pleasure and the use of public libraries. In 2018, the initiative saw 655,076 children take part in the challenge and the Beano-inspired theme proved popular and provided significant scope for activities as the following feedback from a parent in Kirklees authority shows: 'I really loved the theme this year, and the brightly coloured Beano materials. The Mischief Makers idea was fun, and the library organised lots of really good events using the theme. One of the best years yet!' (The Reading Agency, 2018).

Primary Education advisers Lindsey Pickton and Christine Chen (2019) wrote about the immersive power of comics on the teacher resource website, 'Teach Wire', commenting that 'by connecting to their on-screen experience of cartoon and movies, comics allow children to immerse themselves independently in whole stories, with illustrations throwing light on unfamiliar vocabulary.'

Primary Times suggests some activities that can easily translate to library settings and can work as part of ChatterBooks sessions or as holiday activities:

- Use a panel of a comic strip as a 'freeze frame' and encourage students to thought-track the characters in the frame, tapping each participant to unfreeze them and have them say what they are thinking and feeling at that moment in the story.
- Use a comic panel or strips with the speech bubbles blanked out so that children can be encouraged to create their own dialogue to help make sense of the story that the illustrations are showing.

Comic characters can also create promotional opportunities. Using the *2000 AD* character 'Judge Dredd' as a base, one of the teenage reading groups I worked with at a public library in Preston explored the idea of 'Judge Read', a library based character. They thought through what outfit he might wear, the types of powers and vulnerabilities he might have. This acted as an access point for encouraging the reading group to explore a different type of literature to that which they had previously encountered.

Alongside developing reading, encountering a wide range of comic book artists and styles can help to stimulate creation. Gene Luen Yang (2019), winner of the Printz award for his graphic novel *American Born Chinese*, is a lecturer on graphic novels and comics and holder of the National Ambassador for Young People's Literature post in America (2016–17). Here he talks about the form and some of the creators that have gone on to influence his work:

INFLUENCES AND INSIGHTS 83

Comics are as varied as pebbles on a beach and among these can be found a wealth of appropriate literature – from *Captain Underpants*, to graphic novels and, the all-time favourite: *Beano*. Readers will often choose stories featuring familiar characters like Dennis the Menace or Minnie the Minx, forming favourites over time. For many young readers, comics are the first type of text they turn to voluntarily; this isn't surprising as the visual storytelling makes them accessible to the developing reader.

I just love how the comics medium combines words and images. The image between the two can be very complex. They can support one another. They can contradict one another. They can pass the narrative responsibility back and forth. The magic of the medium is in that complexity. Graphic novels that have influenced my work include: *Bone* by Jeff Smith, *Adolf* by Osamu Tezuka and *One Hundred Demons* by Lynda Barry.

Graphic novels

Although graphic novels and comics have acquired significant, often cult, audiences, being aside from the mainstream, artist and writer Bryan Talbot (2019) discusses the complexities of categorising the form and considers some of its history:

'Graphic novel' is a marketing term for the format of comics in book form, first used as such in 1978 in the marketing of Will Eisner's *A Contract with God*. As the book was an anthology of three short stories, rather than a novel, it was a misnomer from the word go. Many of today's graphic novels are autobiographical or factual, leading to the nonsensical marketing term 'non-fiction graphic novels'. Because people tend to know what it means, I use 'graphic novels' to describe the books that I write and draw, but I don't care for it.

The term 'graphic novel' is inadequate and misleading. 'Graphic', with its connotations of both commercial art and explicit pornographic or violent images, is followed by 'novel', suggesting that it's a bastard offspring of another art form, that of prose fiction, which it patently isn't. The comic medium has its own distinct history, traditions and grammar and predates the novel form. 'Novel' also indicates a length that many graphic novels don't have; most graphic novels are actually novellas or short stories, such as Alan Moore's *The Killing Joke*.

Moore simply calls his books 'big comics', partly to deflate any claims of pretension but chiefly to irritate proponents of the 'graphic novel' label. But this is also problematic. For one thing, 'comics' describes the entire medium, from the three-panel gag strip to Moore's and Eddie Campbell's scholarly epic *From Hell*, so a 'big comic' could just as easily mean a sequential mural or a six-foot high comic page. Secondly, the word 'comic' itself is a misnomer, dating back to the mid-nineteenth century's 'comic (meaning funny) supplements' and 'comic companions' to newspapers and, as we know, graphic novels often deal with tragedy. Like 'comics', 'sequential art' is unspecific and also a bit of a mouthful, as is 'pictorial narrative'. So it looks as though we're stuck with the phrase 'graphic novel', or its equally unsatisfactory and even less descriptive abbreviation, 'GN'.

In the mid-1980s, the first boom of GNs, spearheaded by Art Spiegelman's *Maus*, Moore and Gibbon's *Watchmen* and Frank Miller's *Dark Knight Returns*, seemed like the dawn of a new age. Respectable newspapers and grown-up magazines ran features on them. Comics were suddenly cool. But it didn't last. There simply wasn't the quantity and range of quality books to build on the nascent public interest. Instead, capitalising on the growing demand, opportunistic comic book publishers compiled handfuls of monthly production-line superhero titles and released them as 'graphic novels'. Duped readers expecting another *Watchmen* were predictably disappointed and these books confirmed their old prejudices about comics.

Since then, however, graphic novels have been produced seemingly exponentially to such an extent that there is now a large canon of quality graphic novels, in every conceivable genre and art style, enough to sustain this second boom. We are living in a golden age of GNs. There are now more and better graphic novels in print than ever before. From Joe Sacco's reportage to Jeff Smith's comedy adventure, from Ed Brubaker and Sean Phillip's macho noir to Marjane Satrapi's poignancy, from the realism of Harvey Pekar to the fantasy of Neil Gaiman. Graphic novels about social issues, history, politics and biography abound.

In sharp contrast to the insular boys' locker-room world of comic shops prior to the revolution, public libraries and mainstream bookstores now have graphic novel sections and, according to the marketing director of Barnes and Noble, the GN is the fastest growing area of book sales in the last hundred years. People who wouldn't consider themselves 'comic fans' are now reading GNs. Every respectable book festival has a graphic novel component and graphic novels even win literary awards. Chris Ware's *Jimmy Corrigan* won the Guardian Book Award, *Dotter of Her Father's Eyes*, written by my wife, Mary Talbot, won the Costa Biography Award and *Sabrina* by Nick Drnaso was shortlisted for that holy of holies – The Booker Prize.

The graphic novel is a form whose time has come and is here to stay.

Twice winner of the CILIP Kate Greenaway medal, Raymond Briggs, works on a column for *The Oldie*, here he speaks compellingly about the art snobbery associated with illustration and cartoons in his book *Notes from the Sofa* (2015), pointing out the heightened cultural appreciation for the comic strip or Bande Dessinée which occurs on the continent:

Below painting comes Illustration. Oh, dear. The very word is used as a pejorative. The worst thing you can say about a painting is that it is 'illustrative'. If the painter hears you, he will kill you. This, despite the world renowned names of John Tenniel, Beatrix Potter, and E. H. Shepard.

Below them comes Cartoons. Here we are virtually in the gutter press, despite Carl Giles and David Low. Admittedly, he eventually became Sir David Low. No doubt the government was trying to butter up the proprietor.

Then, below the gutter, are the sewers – Strip Cartoons! Comics! Ugh! The very cesspits of non-culture, read by utterly common people such as children, foreigners and Americans.

On the continent, Bande Dessinée is a respected medium, just as important as Theatre and Film. They call it Ninth Art. In Japan, Manga are published in their millions.

Now at last, the Graphic Novel has attained dignity and respect in this country. Thanks mainly to Jonathan Cape, Britain is at last waking up to this centuries-old art form. Recently, there was a presentation about the Graphic Novel at the I.C.A. Soon there is to be a similar event at the Royal Society of Literature. Steven Spielberg wants to make a multimillion-dollar movie of *Tintin*. Both Ian Rankin and Philip Pullmun are writing for the medium.

Respect! About time, too.

In the information age when so much data is available instantaneously through the internet, the ways in which some of these relationships operate is likely to change, but there is little doubt in such a visual arena that illustration and graphics will continue to play a seminal role.

CHAPTER 5

Windows into Worlds: the importance of visual representation and inclusion

Visual literacy offers readers the opportunity to literally see themselves reflected in the visual texts that they encounter. This can be enormously empowering, showing that reading is inclusive and embraces a wide range of life experiences and backgrounds, affirming many different identities. For professionals working with books, whether in schools, libraries or bookshops, this means attention should be paid to ensure that representation in their book stock is not outmoded or problematic. Just as society shifts and progresses over time, so too does our understanding of what it means to be inclusive and how best to achieve this. Despite the immediacy that visual representation allows, as part of an overall collection, the inclusivity and authenticity of what is being represented can be easy to overlook.

Encountering a wide range of characters with varying backgrounds and lifestyles can be an effective means for helping to normalise situations and increase exposure to a broad range of experiences from an early age. Illustrations within the books we read are able to convey subtle messages that can enrich and at times challenge societal conventions, taking an active role without this needing to be part of the main narrative of the story and thereby feeling didactic. An example of this might include two characters of the same sex holding hands whilst taking a child to school; the inclusion of children wearing glasses, hearing aids or other support equipment in classroom scenes; or a range of different cultures being represented.

This chapter explores different facets of diversity and lived experience and how these can be represented visually in books in ways that are respectful, contemporary and authentic, helping to ensure that books are inclusive and reflect the society they are part of.

Cultural diversity

Signifiers of different cultures can be embedded into visual narratives in a variety of ways. Broadly, this may include skin-tone, hair-colour and hair type but can also be referenced through subtle details, such as the foods that characters are depicted as eating, the textiles and clothing that they wear, or the environment they are located within.

In appraising visual representation in books, it is important to look out for caricatures, where physical attributes are exaggerated in ways that perpetuate stereotypes and to consider when the book was published as books from a certain age are likely to depict a view of people which is influenced by the politics of the day. An example of this is *Tintin in the Congo* a graphic novel featuring the eponymous boy journalist and written and illustrated by Herge. The depiction of the people and landscape of the Congo in this graphic novel drew upon limited source material, much of this steeped in colonial viewpoints. This is reflected in the style of illustration which led to criticism of the book's publication in colour in the UK in 2005. Discussion ensued about whether the book should be removed from sale or whether it represented an important part of societal history and progress. There is a danger that wiping out books of this kind leads to making history anodyne, but equally it's important to contextualise these limited and outdated portrayals through raising awareness of the visual representations of culture that counter these stereotypes. If outdated representation constitutes the only opportunity for readers to encounter particular cultures, this endangers perpetuating stereotypes.

Central to conversations around authentic representation of culture and diverse experience is who is telling the story. Discourse around own voices, recognising the way artists record and relay the culture and groups that they are a part of can be a powerful way to communicate representation that is informed and nuanced. It is important to ensure that representation is not at the exclusion of those who come from particular cultures or groups, indeed people with lived experience of what is being represented should be a part of constructing these stories.

Illustrator, Yu Rong (2019), discusses her approach to illustration and the manner in which this is rooted in Chinese traditions, a hybridisation of different cultural approaches:

> I was inspired by Chinese paper cut which was created a long, long time ago, it is in a two dimensional flat form, mostly in the colour red with

topics focused on farming, people use them to decorate windows and doors to celebrate festivals. Studying at the Royal College of Art, I freed my mind of thinking, thus leading me to explore the possibilities for how to use paper cut to convey my ideas into artwork. Through decades of practice, I have learned how to use the characteristic of paper cut to fully express my creative ideas. It is fun, spontaneous and unique. My journey has turned the use of paper cut technique passively to a more positive free method.

Figure 5.1 *Traditional papercut illustration from Shu Lin's Grandpa by Yu Rong.* Image reproduced with kind permission of Otter-Barry Books © Yu Rong, 2019

In selecting titles as part of collections, it is imperative to be aware of the role unconscious bias can play in these decisions. Unconscious bias is the way the brain creates shortcuts and tends to favour that which it is already familiar or comfortable with. This can act as an impediment to achieving a representative collection.

Likewise, when choosing core titles for a collection, it is important consider the effects of colonisation that often impacts upon canonical titles. There has been significant work into decolonisation of the classroom, which has extended to collections in the library. Creating an inclusive collection in the library is key area to ensuring a representative and wide reaching base for all readers. Thinking around who the primary audience of the collection is perceived to be and considering the types of world view represented by the books is an important starting point in this.

Cultural influences can affect an illustrator or artist's artwork and when executed successfully can lend a sense of authenticity to the visuals created, as well as providing access to styles and techniques from other countries and cultures. Illustrator Poonam Mistry (2019) discusses some of the influences behind her work:

> My artwork is greatly influenced by Indian folk art and textiles but also other forms of traditional art celebrated around the world. As my style is heavily decorative, it's important that the image itself remains simple and encapsulates what the text is trying to say in its basic form. Each layer of pattern is almost a piece of thread and together they weave and entwine to create a tapestry of different elements and images that feels unified and one. The patterns I draw often curve and adjust to the shape of animals and organic forms to help create movement and fluidity. For me, it is important that my style reflects my heritage and roots. It helps to give the reader an idea of who is behind the pictures.

A powerful way to help curate a representative collection – where selection processes enable this – is to work with a consultative group of young people trying to ensure that this comprises of individuals with a range of lived experience. As visual narratives are often more immediate, this can be an effective way both of giving voice to young people and visibility to underrepresented groups.

Gender

There are tendencies for lead characters in picturebooks to be presented as male regardless as to whether those leads are human, animal or toys. In 2018 and 2019, *The Observer* in the United Kingdom analysed the top selling 100 picturebooks in 2017. Analysis found that characters depicted as male were twice as likely to have speaking roles as their female counterparts and that in 20% of books females were excluded (Day, 2018). Little changed in 2018 with readers 1.6 times as likely to read a picturebook from the list with a male rather than a female protagonist and seven times more likely to encounter a male villain than a female villain (Fergusson, 2019). Although these statistics are limited to the top 100 bestselling picturebooks, a fact industry professionals criticised as this excludes around 66% of publishing output (Eyre, 2019b), they nonetheless show systemic issues whereby titles which challenge these 'norms' do not get the same profile or likely marketing spend, often coming from smaller independent publishers. There is a role for librarians, educators and booksellers to proactively seek titles which buck this trend, helping to positively affirm changes both in attitude and creating better visibility for titles which are less gendered.

These issues are not confined to the United Kingdom, a 2011 Florida State University study led by Janice McCabe, assistant professor of sociology, explored 6,000 books published from 1900 to 2000 and found male central characters were present in 57% of children's books publishing per year, while only 31% had female central characters (McCabe et al., 2011). Why does gender representation remain so skewed? The 1976 publication *Sexism in Children's Books* outlined issues that remain current today: 'an examination of prize-winning picturebooks reveals that women are greatly under-represented in the titles, central roles and illustrations. Where women do appear their characterisation reinforces traditional sex-role stereotypes: boys are active while girls are passive: boys lead and rescue others while girls follow and serve others' (Weitzman et al., 1976).

What are termed 'traditional sex-role stereotypes' continue to abound in visual representations and it's important to recognise where this happens. Established classics like Judith Kerr's *The Tiger Who Came to Tea* show traditional gender roles with the father coming in from work and the mum doing the cooking and washing up. Books continue to be published which unquestioningly show 'dad's toolbox' and mum's knitting, or mum cooking and dad driving, perpetuating images of patriarchal leadership and dominance and mums often being exclusively in roles as homemakers. Achieving a balance through collections is a key way to challenge pervasive stereotypes and the role of librarians and booksellers in providing access and focus for titles with less marketing spend is vitally important.

Alongside books which continue to promote limiting stereotypes of gender, there are also titles that have been produced in a specifically gendered way, such as colouring books for boys with blue covers and footballs and books for girls that are pink and feature fairies and princesses. Several publishers have now agreed to stop designing and publishing titles in this way. Jessica Love (2019), author and illustrator of *Julian is a Mermaid* a lithe exploration of gender stereotyping which won the Klaus Flugge Prize in 2019, explains why she feels diversity is something of a misnomer:

> In some ways I think 'diversity' is a misnomer, and 'reality' might be more appropriate. For a long time the world of published books in the West hasn't reflected the human race, only a very narrow sliver of it. What we've seen depicted has been some bizarro world in which everyone is white, skinny, English speaking, young, able-bodied, wealthy...the list goes on. For everyone who wasn't white/able-bodied/slim/English-speaking this paradigm communicated the message: you don't exist. But I believe that paradigm is equally damaging to the narrow sliver of the population that *was* depicted because it reinforced the extremely dangerous idea that their experience was the one that counted – and I cannot think of a more poisonous seed to plant in a young person's mind. The kids who never got to see themselves in books deserve to see themselves represented in stories. And the kids who see depictions of themselves everywhere they go need an opportunity to identify with characters who look and sound nothing like them – empathy is a muscle and stories are the best workout there is.

Sexuality

A range of sexual identities can be presented through illustrative texts. This might be in the form of board books for the very young like Todd Parr's *The Family Book*, which depicts all manner of different family types including showing family units made up with two mothers and two fathers. Books like this help to positively present different family types but through merely depicting these, offer no kind of comment, simply allowing readers the opportunity to witness different family units.

Graphic novels allow for more sophisticated exploration like Tom Bouden's graphic novel, *Max and Sven*, which through the *ligne claire* – clear line – style of graphic novels allows feelings and experiences of adolescent sexual awakenings to be conveyed, or similarly, see Alice Oseman's *Heartstopper*.

Mental health

After years of stigma, a greater awareness of mental health and its reach within society is driving a need for published titles that uncover and unpick these areas of human experience. Conditions around mental health can feel inescapable and overwhelming regardless of the stage of life when this occurs. Finding a common language to express this can be particularly challenging making experience all the more isolating, particularly for the young with more limited vocabulary.

By providing direct and raw access to emotion and feeling through visual representation, meaning can be conveyed in ways that are easily accessible and understandable for those who have mental health or wellbeing needs, or those who encounter these in their relationships with others. Books like Eva Eland's *When Sadness Comes to Call* adeptly use poise and palette to relay the pervasive nature of sadness. This is true too of Debi Gliori's *Night Shift*, which was informed by Debi's personal struggles with depression. *Night Shift* received wide readership among a variety of age groups, showcasing that picturebooks do not have to be for the very young and are capable of sustaining complex and sophisticated themes.

Speaking with Debi (2019) about *Night Shift*, she discusses how visual literacy can help us to create recognition and understanding for situations and emotions that we all may experience at different points in our lives:

> *Night Shift* wasn't meant to be a book. Not at first. It began with a desire on my part to communicate what it feels like to suffer from depressive illness. I wasn't sure who I wanted to communicate with; mainly my family, I guess, but also, probably myself. Sick of trying to encapsulate the experience of depression, I found I was running out of language. Or, language was running out of me, but none of it was accurate.
>
> Words weren't working, they failed to convey just how bleak and lonely the territory was. Can be. Actually, is.
>
> So I picked up a stick of charcoal and without preamble or any planning whatsoever, began to draw how I felt. To map the territory. And to my surprise, I found that the act of drawing without constraint or deadline, with the possibility that nobody would ever see what I'd made, was immensely liberating. The drawings flowed, one after the other, in no particular order.
>
> Without words, the drawings spoke clearly. They spoke a universal language, leaving space for individual interpretation without misunderstanding. When I had amassed a pile of black, smudgy, heartfelt drawings, I realised, much to my surprise that I had made a book. I was and am hugely grateful to the team of dedicated professionals who took that pile of drawings and turned it into the finished version of *Night Shift*.

Empathy

Empathy, the ability to better understand and to share in the experiences or feelings of others, is often key to considerations of diversity and inclusion. Illustrations can be an excellent way to foster empathy as character's emotions are often easy to infer through their facial expressions and poise. Eva Eland (2019), author and illustrator of *When Sadness Comes to Call* talks about empathy and the ability illustrations hold in unlocking aspects of our inner lives:

> It was very important for me to make this book as accessible and universal as possible, and at the same time also to create a meaningful reading experience that people could relate to on a personal level. I think the paired back text and illustrations allow for some space where the reader is invited to reflect on his or her own experiences and relationship with sadness. Books can give us opportunities to recognise ourselves and to feel seen, especially those parts that we tend to suppress and hide for ourselves and others. Comforted by the knowledge that we aren't alone – we might find more compassion for these often overlooked parts of ourselves.

The concept of illustration is, in many ways, built around ideas of empathy as it is key that pictures meaningfully sit alongside and extend the feelings and mood of the story or text. Winner of the former UNESCO Other award, *Something Else* written by Kathryn Cave and illustrated by Chris Riddell is an excellent example of how this can be achieved. The book focuses upon a creature that does not look like or easily fit in with others. The illustrations visually signpost this through the positioning of the character of Something Else; readers are introduced to the creature when he is facing away from them, looking into a mirror, we see from his reflection that he is downcast and isolated. The other creatures directly face the readers with closed body language, often with hands in pockets and raised eyebrows. Poise, position on the page, facial expression and body language all visually help to signify the thoughts and emotions of characters thereby enabling us to better understand and have compassion for them.

Learning needs

Illustration can be a powerful tool to support readers with learning needs. In 2002, the National Autistic Society published a paper exploring the relationship between *Thomas the Tank Engine* and children with autistic spectrum disorder. A survey of 81 parents of children with autism and Asperger syndrome was conducted to explore the relationship between their children and the character of Thomas. Findings showed that 57% of children on the autistic spectrum associated with Thomas before other children's characters they encountered, that the character constituted a point of entry for skills around communication and learning. The report states 'children with autism often respond well to visual impact. One-to-one teaching, because it involves an element of social interaction, can be stressful and problematic.' The report also identified the usefulness of the still backgrounds and scenery, which does not distract, and found that the faces of the engines that feature exaggerated expressions aided understanding. One parent commented, 'without doubt it is the faces on each engine which first attracted his interest. The expression on the faces never changes and he knows they won't talk back to him!'

Visual appeal through design and illustration can help create accessible books for readers with dyslexia. In design terms, fonts which help to reduce visual stress are sans script, those without extensions or 'serifs' at the end of the letterforms. Larger font sizes can be helpful as can greater spacing between letters and words to avoid over-crowding. Underlining, italics and text in uppercase can contribute to the letters or words running together making this hard to read. Illustrations can help to break up large passages of text aiding readability. Some illustrated texts use hand-lettering and typographical effect to such a high extent that they can be almost impenetrable for dyslexic readers. Awareness and caution should be taken to avoid placing text upon very busy backgrounds or using colours that are likely to over-stimulate. Lightly tinted paper can often help to reduce letters running into one another. Likewise, some graphic novels use hand-lettered uppercase fonts in speech bubbles which makes readability hard for readers with dyslexia. It is important to consider these visual aspects when reviewing book stock to achieve a balanced, inclusive and accessible collection.

Inclusion

Visually representing different physical attributes, whether that be height, age, body size or different types of adaptive equipment such as glasses, hearing aids, wheelchairs, crutches, callipers, can be a powerful way of showcasing inclusion. Pictures enable these diverse attributes to be incorporated subtly a part of groups and scenes. It is also possible to show inclusion through accessible environments whether that be ramps for wheelchair access, depicting grab rails, textured and high contrast pavements to support the visually impaired, or wheelchair friendly lifts as well as staircases. All of this can be a powerful way to affirm a range of life experiences helping under-represented groups to feel included rather than excluded.

A project run by the disability and equality charity Scope called 'In the Picture' aimed at raising awareness among publishers and illustrators about making visual literacy more inclusive. Alex Strick (n.d.) who led on the project provides some handy hints on what to look for in inclusive illustrations.

Things to look for in inclusive illustrations

1. Are disabled characters included in a natural way, this means including characters within the book but recognising disability is for many just a natural part of daily life. This can be achieved subtly through including characters in group scenes without particular reference or highlighting.
2. Look out for characters that offer stereotyped representations. It can often be that portrayal of characters with disabilities can over-compensate through creating powers or abilities that can seem superhuman. Be wary too of stereotypes where the most popular or attractive characters are presented in a wholly idealised way.
3. Are different forms of disability represented and are these across all ages. Many people see disability as synonymous with being a wheelchair user, but there are many groups who are under-represented including people who are deaf, partially sighted or with learning needs. It is often difficult to find positive representation of adults with disability in children's books too, so look out for titles that show characters with positive careers, relationships and children.
4. Think carefully about the way equipment and adapted environments are presented to tie with particular character's needs.
5. Look out for representation of less visible conditions like dyslexia where characters might be wearing tinted glasses, or characters who are deaf and might be using sign language.

This kind of positive inclusive work can be seen in practice in many library settings. For example, Alison Brumwell whilst working for Kirklees Bookplus, partnered with the Kirklees transcription service to develop boxed resources to support learning opportunities and materials for partially sighted children. These resources included examples of braille and Moon, tactile maps and illustrations and audio materials alongside puppets, musical instruments and smaller objects from the service's collection. This was a simple and effective way of ensuring inclusion and accessibility for learning at the library.

Sight

Decoding visual literacy can be challenged or even limited by visual impairment or lack of sight. This can be aided by various supportive apparatus, including magnifying lenses or enlargement equipment and for children with lower levels of sight, the use of high contrast and bright colours can mean that illustrations and images are able to be accessed.

In online environments, use of alt text (alternative text), can describe images enabling screen readers to understand the image based upon text descriptions used. The charity, Living Paintings was founded in 1989 by Alison Oldland, a former lecturer in art history, with the aim of providing people who are partially sighted or blind with the opportunity to engage with art. The charity initially provided a range of art and leisure books for adults with a model that brought together tactile illustrations and audio descriptions. The charity grew to create projects which would support children in enjoying picturebooks and having access to educational resources for use both at home and in school with similar tactile and audio books. The charity is a free postal lending library for anyone in the United Kingdom who is blind or partially sighted including, schools, health authorities and care homes as well as individuals.

The charity ClearVision creates braille interleaved picturebooks which enable access for readers who are blind but also that facilitate book-sharing for parents or carers who are blind and have sighted children. The books feature the text and descriptions of illustration in braille and are created on transparent interleaves in a way that enables print and braille to be read simultaneously.

ClearVision also hold a library of tactile books. Whereas several commercially available board books feature tactile elements, these often do not adequately meet the needs of children who have impaired vision as the single tactile element on each page rarely has sufficient context to be meaningful. The tactile books stocked by ClearVision provide a more complete reading experience allowing for the development of a story arc or else for information to be conveyed. One of the ways ClearVision is able to collect titles of this kind is through entries for the International Typhlo & Tactus Award. Established in 1999, this award is run annually and, at the time of writing this book has 23 countries participating. Tactile book making can be a targeted and focused activity for craft groups in libraries and is a useful way to learn about the mechanics of how stories and information can be conveyed across books, whilst helping to build provision for an area not currently represented through mainstream commercial publishing. Find out more by visiting their website www.clearvisionproject.org.

ClearVision Project: The Six S's

ClearVision recommends thinking about their six S's, ensuring that books produced are:

1. **Safe** – ensuring all elements are securely attached and there are not elements that might pose a health and safety risk to children.
2. **Simple** – determining things by touch can be difficult, keeping things simple and testing these can be useful to ensure suitability.
3. **Small** – children have small hands and laps so small books are best suited to them. ClearVision recommends pages not being longer than 25cm by 25cm and also suggest books should open out flat to allow ease of exploration.
4. **Short** – using touch to explore the pages takes time, it is recommended books do not exceed 8–10 pages.
5. **Sturdy** – even careful exploration results in quite robust handling and not all children have finely developed motor skills. It is important to make sure all items are well attached.
6. **Stimulating** – varying textures, rough and smooth, hard and soft, warm and cold can be effective as can introducing sounds and smells. Bold colour contrasts and shiny and sparkling elements can help to stimulate children with low vision.

Source: *Making Tactile Books for the ClearVision Library*, www.clearvisionproject.org/resources/Tactile-book-makers-guide.pdf

---

An additional resource to be aware of is the 'Picture Books Plus Foundation' (https://prentenboekenplus.nl/en). The project aims to develop and publish picturebooks for children with visual impairments utilising a range of tactile graphics and braille with the aim to prepare children for reading comprehension. The book sets also include a three-dimensional object relating to the story.

Case study 5.1   Linden Lodge Tactile Wall

Multi-award winning author Anne Fine (2019) talks about the creation of a tactile wall at Linden Lodge School. This was one of the projects she spearheaded during her time as Children's Laureate in 2001–03.

I think the first time I realised that children who are blind or seriously visually impaired lack the constant and daily stimulus the rest of us take for granted was when I visited two blind parents with newborn sighted twins. No pictures on the nursery walls. No decorations round or above the cots. Happily, next time I saw the room, the health visitor had dealt with that!

The second most striking occasion was moving from giving a morning talk in a typical school library, replete with posters and bright book jackets facing outwards, to an afternoon talk in a boarding school for the blind. This was a long time ago, but I well remember the plain walls and the acres of biblical looking brailled tomes, all covered in the same sturdy brown paper.

When I became Laureate in 2001, I was determined to include blind and seriously visually impaired children. And along with all the other schemes we used to drawn them in, we had The Tactile Wall.

The idea came out of the blue. I walk my dog with a retired architect, Angus Forsyth, who keeps a lathe in his basement and works with wood as a hobby. Angus talked about what he was making for a nearby nursery, where the smallest children took naps on mats. 'I've made a tactile frieze along the wall, low down. Snail shell pattern indentations they can run their fingers round and round; half-filled hot water bottle cases fixed to the wall that they can "flob" over and over; short dowelling rods they can push in to make another pop out. Nothing colourful to encourage them to keep their eyes open,' he said. 'Just something they can *feel* as they relax.'

'I know who needs that,' I told him.

Angus designed the tactile wall for Linden Lodge School as if it were a bus shelter. It stood on four sturdy legs fixed in the ground. It was three sided for stability, wind protection and easy roof coverage. It offered tactile experiences of all sorts inside and out at every height – some involving a partner on the other side, some not. It was set on wheelchair-friendly ground.

It is astonishing how many – and how much – things can 'feel' different. Compare string, rope, tassels, embroidery silks, wool and cotton. Compare warm wood with cold steel. Once you get thinking, you'll run out of space to house all your ideas, even after you junk all of the ones that won't be safe and temper tantrum proof.

To all the different tactile amusements, we added sections that could make interesting sounds – bells, clicks, fart noises – anything to stimulate or amuse, keeping them to a volume that wouldn't drive everyone around stark mad. But it was interesting to see how often the children who used it, many of whom have other problems apart from poor vision, returned to tracing the various finger patterns and mazes on the squares. I suppose they found them endlessly comforting in the way twisting your hair compulsively around your fingers is soothing.

Materials aren't costly, since a lot of them are offcuts, or recycled. Local clubs and charities usually know someone who can help, not just with what fundraising is needed, but with the wood or metal working skills. (You'll find some retired council employee who knows how to put up a weird sort of bus shelter safely and securely.) We made Linden Lodge's tactile wall as three separate sides in County Durham, and drove it down to South London to be fixed together there.

Wait till you see the photos of children using it. It will make all the effort more than worthwhile.

Colour blindness

Colour vision deficiency, or colour blindness to use its common term, affects roughly 8% of men and 0.5% of women globally. Most people who have the condition have acquired it genetically, although it can be acquired through aging. Colour blindness can be tested by opticians. It can affect the way readers engage with visual texts. Picturebook author and illustrator, Steve Antony (2019), talks about his condition and how this affects his illustration:

People are often surprised to discover that I'm red-green colourblind. But it really isn't all that unusual. In fact, I know a couple of other children's book illustrators who are also red-green colourblind. As a child, I really struggled to pick the right coloured pencils or paints, but that never deterred me from following my dream to become a children's book illustrator. Even now, I often second-guess my ability to colour-in my pencil drawings. This is why I often use very limited colour palettes or approach colour in an abstract or conceptual way. But if not for my colour-blindness my books would look totally different, and I actually enjoy the challenge of working with very few colours. In my *Mr Panda* series, the characters are all black and white animals: a penguin, a lemur, a killer whale and so on. As a result, the doughnuts and other coloured-in props really stand out. For *The Queen's Hat*, my first picture book, I used only red, white and blue (and some black) the colours of the Union Jack, which made perfect sense. For the sequel, *The Queen's Handbag*, I used the same colours but this time I reversed them so that the characters, mainly police officers chasing the Queen, were all in blue as opposed to red, which the Queen's guards wore in the first instalment. The third in the series, *The Queen's Present*, is made up of festive reds and greens (this was particularly challenging).

More recently I've started stepping out my comfort zone by using more colours in books like *When I Grow Up*, *Unplugged*, and *Amazing*. But my colour choices are never haphazard or spontaneous; every selection of colour is intentional.

What I've learned is that the sky doesn't have to be blue and grass doesn't have to be green. Artists can pick whatever colours they want. After all, art is all about self-expression. I guess I made up my own rules, instead of referring to colour wheels, popular swatches or photographs. By doing so I've developed a way of working that is fun, satisfying and rewarding.

With many inclusive and diverse titles being published by smaller, independent publishers, they face a challenge in generating profile and visibility for these titles as they often do not receive the same marketing or publicity spend as titles published to be overtly commercially. *Pen&inc.* is a new magazine and listings guide for diverse and inclusive children's books produced by CILIP, the library and information association, who govern the Carnegie and Kate Greenaway Awards. The magazine is sent to all CILIP members, to booksellers and to library authorities. The magazine grew out of the lack of representation in the UK children's publishing market and an awareness that the supply system can mean that some titles do not get the same level of profile or visibility as others. The publication creates listings and offers profile opportunities for smaller presses. Features within the magazine allow focus to be created around underrepresented creators and the cover has been used as a chance to showcase illustration. Cate Simmonds (2019) from 'News from Nowhere Radical and Community Bookshop' discusses the value she has got out of *Pen&inc.* as a bookseller:

I do quite a lot of the researching and ordering of our children's book stock, and we deliberately try to always have titles on our shelves that are inclusive, and which represent a really diverse range of characters and subjects (these are the subject areas we either stock, or can order).
Having *Pen&inc.* is a huge help, as (even just from a brief initial browse) I'm finding titles that we didn't know existed, and would definitely like to stock. It's a fantastic resource and a great read – and I really appreciate the obvious time and care that's gone into compiling it.

Historically, increasing representation in children's books has been difficult to embed in the long-term, with initiatives blossoming but fading away as diversity and inclusion is treated like a trend rather than an essential part of the children's book landscape. To increase visual representation and embed lasting change, it requires all involved in the book trade to work together to ensure that obstacles and barriers are identified and removed where possible so that all children have the opportunity to see books and reading as inviting and involving themselves.

CHAPTER 6

Prize-winning Pictures: an exploration of awards and honours

Awards can be a powerful way to give profile to particular books and artists and to help incite interest and momentum in reading. Awards also play a valuable role in helping to document and record implicit cultural views on childhood, educational perspectives on reading and learning and the practices and processes of professions associated with books and reading – publishers, authors, illustrators, librarians and booksellers. They offer insight into the development of the field and the principles adhered to and valued within these. Awards can play a particularly important role for visual narratives as they place a weight of value and importance upon illustration and artwork helping to show the worth of the form overall. Awards for new illustrators can also provide access points for new talent, an important consideration for an industry that can be challenging to enter.

There are numerous international, national and regional awards for illustration. Books that are shortlisted or that win major awards can see an up-turn in sales and can influence future publishing decisions. In an age when the majority of library stock is decided through supplier selection, awards can play a key role in librarians staying up to date, keeping abreast of new talent and themes or trends that might be emerging both nationally and internationally.

Awards also offer opportunities to engage children and young people through national reading groups and shadowing schemes, or through regionally run initiatives that seek to promote reading for pleasure. Awards provide an opportunity to gain professional awareness of some of the most highly regarded titles being published. This chapter explores international, national and local book awards outlining their background, process and notable winners. Particular focus is given to the CILIP Kate Greenaway Medal as I currently chair the working party for this award and with its shadowing scheme for children and young people it has considerable national and international reach.

The CILIP Kate Greenaway Medal

Winning the Kate Greenaway Medal, and later the 'Greenaway of Greenaways', for my picture book *Dogger*, was an enormous honour, particularly as it is awarded by highly regarded professional librarians. When I first started out, after illustrating many books, mostly in line, by other authors, I was told that my books were 'too English' to be readily accepted abroad. But it turns out that children all over the world have no problem in taking a story to heart, no matter what the setting, if the plot and pictures really appeal to them.

(Shirley Hughes, 2019)

Awarded for an outstanding reading experience achieved through illustration, the Kate Greenaway Medal was established in 1955 and awarded for the first time in 1956 – the prize was withheld in its first year as it was felt no books in contention were suitable. The award is the longest running and most prestigious children's book award for illustration in the UK. It was won awarded for the first time in 1956 to Edward Ardizzone for *Tim All Alone*. The origins of the award date back to Harold Jones who received a commendation for his illustrations for the book *Lavender's Blue*, a collection of nursery rhymes. At this point discussions had been held around the important role that illustration can play in terms of children's books and reading and the role a prestigious illustration award could play in stimulating the creation of more outstanding illustrated works for children.

Process

Judged by a panel of librarians from CILIP's Youth Libraries Group, the award is very much the profession's prize. Each September nominations open and members of CILIP are invited to nominate a title that they feel is deserving of the Medal. Regional sub-committees of the Youth Libraries Group play an active role in coordinating nominations and identifying titles throughout the year that meet the criteria. There is no age limit for books that are nominated but they must have been published on a children's list.

There are between twelve and fourteen judges on the panel each year – twelve representing the different regions of the UK and the opportunity for a further two to be co-opted if additional representation is needed on the panel.

Nominated books are checked for eligibility and judges are expected to read all of the books put forward, appraising them against the criteria and meeting to discuss each title with the panel before drawing up a longlist of no more than twenty books. After close exploration and discussion of the longlist, a shortlist of no more than eight books is selected. After the shortlisted books are announced, children and young people 'shadow' the awards process, reading and debating the books before selecting their own winner which is announced alongside the Kate Greenaway Medal winner that the judges choose after re-reading and deliberating upon the titles.

Notable winners include:

Chris Riddell has won the award more times than anyone in the history of the Medal, with three wins.

Jim Kay's illustrations for *Monsters of Men*, written by Patrick Ness, was the first book to win both the Carnegie and the Kate Greenaway Medal.

Jackie Morris won the 2019 Medal for *The Lost Words*, which was created in response to the removal of numerous words from the Oxford Junior Illustrated Dictionary and notable as it is one of few occasions when the Shadowers' Choice Award (see below) matched with the Medal winner selected by the judging panel.

Shadowing

As mentioned, the awards includes a successful shadowing scheme where reading groups in schools and public libraries read the books, take part in activities and submit their reviews of the shortlisted titles as they gain a deeper understanding of the books, their themes and how the illustrations help to communicate these. Activities include creating artwork inspired by the shortlisted books which can be posted online to the 'Greenaway Gallery'. To take part in the scheme and access further information about the awards and the resources produced to support participation visit www.ckg.org.uk.

Each year, CILIP runs a video competition inviting children to share their shadowing experience and to visually interpret the books they have been reading. The creative responses to these visual texts is inspiring with groups creating their own book covers, collages, paintings and even a memory quilt. The winning shadowing group is invited to attend the award ceremony.

Shadowing groups are encouraged to register their group's favourite book through the website and this contributes towards the overall vote for the Shadowers' Choice award which is announced at the award ceremony. Young people also have the opportunity to present the award on stage to the winning illustrator by taking part in a certificate design competition.

As part of the resources provided for librarians and teachers taking part in the shadowing scheme, the Centre for Literacy in Primary Education (CLPE) and Prue Goodwin create visual literacy notes and teaching ideas. Prue Goodwin (2019) discusses her approach to creating these bespoke resources for the shortlisted books:

> The first statement made in the criteria for any book that wins the Kate Greenaway Medal is that it must be of 'outstanding artistic quality.' As visual texts of all sorts have fascinated me all my career, I was delighted when invited to prepare resources for the groups of students shadowing the Kate Greenaway shortlist. The resources need to offer support to all colleagues – librarians, teachers and a variety of other volunteers – who are shadowing group leaders. Materials also need to be adaptable to different circumstances, taking into account time, group size and facilities (e.g. visualiser, websites etc.) to enable sharing visual texts. Principally, the tasks created are intended to:
>
> - suggest ways of looking and talking about each book
> - encourage close looking to explore different artists' choices of media and their use of colour, shape, line and space on the page
> - help identify how the images enhance a reader's understanding of the text
> - assist critical thinking, discussion and the sharing of individual ideas with the group
> - be adaptable to the strengths of the group and the time available
> - promote active, creative and personal responses.
>
> In order to achieve these intentions, for each book on the shortlist I generally include three sections: looking closely, interpreting the whole text and practical activities. Of course, many group leaders won't need the resources but, for those who do, I hope they provide some useful guidelines towards recognising various ways of identifying 'outstanding artistic quality'.

Amy McKay (2019) School Librarian at Corby Business Academy and Coordinator for the CILIP Carnegie and Kate Greenaway Medals, shadows the awards with four different groups at her school. These groups showcase the broad interest base and appeal that the award generates. Amy commented:

> The Kate Greenaway shadowing is a fantastic scheme that works exceptionally well for a range of students in my school. It's an integral part of our school library calendar and something that both students and staff look forward to every year.
>
> The first group we run Kate Greenaway shadowing with is the bookclub. This group also shadows the Carnegie Medal. The profile for the group tends to be keen readers. Shadowing the Kate Greenaway Medal with them opens up discussion of what an illustrated book is and how to engage with these. In a lot of instances this is with students that might have been told they are past the stage of needing visuals. Shadowing has a huge effect and often the most involved engagement with the books and passionate discussion that occurs within the bookclub is with the Kate Greenaway shortlist. As a sharing experience, it tends to be easier and faster to share the books as it allows interaction and immediate presentation and understanding of themes. It gives the children a good deal of agency as well as the opportunity for different opinions to be shared. Groups often start coming into the library space under their own volition to look at picturebooks in general, running their own ad-hoc storytimes and discussing these. The groups grow because of this with other students eager to join in. They are often keen to look at the backlist of winning authors and to explore the past winners of the award. The shadowing connects them with a love of books that most people have when very young, but that sometimes becomes lost through the education system.

Another group that Amy runs shadowing with is with older students, those in years 10, 11 and at Sixth Form. The approach here is different, although it is still run as a storytime using Kate Greenaway shortlisted titles. At this stage in their school career, the time students can dedicate to reading for pleasure often declines and the aim with the shadowing scheme is to offer a stress free, and non-pressured opportunity to explore books. The library uses this to offer relaxing, sessions that help students to de-stress. It also works as a valuable way of ensuring students continue visiting the library and are reminded that books and reading can be fun as well as purposeful for study. Amy explains:

> There can be some unease among the students when they begin, feeling the books are too young but once they have been to a session they quickly become involved and enjoy it for its own sake, knowing that there is no commitment to turn up, no measures, or expectations to engage, but that they can talk if they wish to and do not have to if not. Students are not encouraged to submit book reviews but know they can if they wish and are able to vote for the books they feel are their favourites, knowing that this contributes to the overall shadowing choice. The scheme is made as low pressure as possible. It is noticeable just how many students who have been involved with the scheme continue to visit and utilise the library after this.

Corby Business Academy also has a Special Educational Needs unit for students with moderate and severe learning difficulties. Whilst these students have specialist teachers and are based within the unit, the school library runs Kate Greenaway shadowing with them. The shortlisted books are likely to be more accessible than other novels because of the illustrations and the initiative offers a way for students to be included in a project that is also part of a mainstream offer and a National scheme. The materials are not differentiated, although the approach and conversations are made appropriate to the target audiences.

> Opinions on the stories tend to be strong and the group gives a platform upon which students really shine. Students are often more receptive in terms of sharing their opinions and in really noticing the details in illustration. The inferences they draw from the pictures and over-arching narratives often delights and surprises the library staff and teachers. With the Ross Collins title, *There's a Bear in my Chair*, (shortlisted for the 2016 Medal), one student who read it, pointed out it was about a sibling and having a baby brother or sister and was able to express why, constructing a compelling argument around this and relating it to his life, showing high level thinking, understanding and empathy. The basis for running the shadowing group is the same as with the other groups run in the library, a general storytime format starts the session with the librarian and the students reading the books together. They use Imprint software in schools and some of the books have symbols, called widgets, on flash cards to help make the stories as accessible

and interactive as possible, giving heightened recognition and enabling input and involvement. The library finds the format is accessible as the visuals of the illustrations do not have to be decoded to access the books.

The final group run in the library is with less confident year seven readers. The Kate Greenaway shortlist and longlist are used because this allows more opportunity for direct involvement. Amy elaborates on this below:

> Once the groups meet, they talk about the books, choose one from the longlist and practice reading, sharing and performing this. The year seven pupils are then encouraged to visit a primary school to do peer reading with reception classes. This builds the confidence of the students who are selected and provides them with a positive experience around books and reading to counter some of the negative ones they might have had in the past. Reading to the reception-aged children is not intimidating and the students are often seen as role models and as being heroes to the primary children. The sessions create a real sense of excitement and joy both among the reception age children and the year sevens that perform the books! Within the Kate Greenaway books there can often be complex language and narrative structures, but the project enables students to engage without fully realising this or feeling dissuaded by it. At the end of the project, the participating students have had a positive experience of the library and feel like they belong there. Many students start borrowing and have lost much of the shame of being a non-reader. The project runs for six weeks in total and by the end of this, average students have seen an increase in their reading age by 4.5 months alongside the accompanying increase in confidence and desire and aptitude to continue reading.

In addition to running the shadowing groups within the school setting, Amy is also instrumental in bring together a town shadowing event, where primary and secondary schools get together to share opinions and celebrate. Alongside providing a spike in engagement and enjoyment of reading, this also provides transition age students at feeder primary schools with experience of the secondary they will move into, giving familiarity and positive early experiences.

Twice winner of the Kate Greenaway Medal, Emily Gravett (2019), discusses the award, reading the reviews by shadowers, and the impact this has had:

Even to be nominated for the Kate Greenaway Medal is immensely exciting, so when my first book *Wolves* went on to be shortlisted, and then subsequently win, it is hard to describe the impact it had not only personally but also professionally. Illustrating can be quite a private activity, so reading the reviews posted by the shadowing scheme was the first time it truly sank in that my book was 'out there' being read.

Professionally I love that the Greenaway Medal recognises the importance of illustration as an integral part of a child's reading experience. As illustrators, we know just how much thought, effort and time goes into the making of a book, so it's great when other people value that effort.

Ultimately making books is about the reader's enjoyment and not winning a prize, but I am convinced that without the Greenaway, my books wouldn't have reached such a wide audience's attention. For parents, teachers etc., it can be hard to choose when faced with a whole shelf of books, so having an endorsement by experts (the librarians of course) can make all the difference to whether a book is picked or not.

The Macmillan Prize for Illustration

The children's book market can be challenging to enter, particularly for new illustrators, as the field is particularly competitive in the United Kingdom. As previously mentioned, it is often required that books be published as co-editions in order to be financially viable. The Macmillan Prize for Children's Picture Book Illustration was established by publisher Macmillan Children's Books in 1985 to help find new talent from illustration schools – the award is also open to all students in higher education establishments in the United Kingdom. Illustrators that have been recognised by the award in the past include Emily Gravett, Bethan Woolvin and Gemma Merino. The award is unusual in that it challenges illustrators to design a complete book.

Process

A judging panel comprising of children's book creators and experts together with members of Macmillan Children's Books, including their Art and Design Director Chris Inns, judge the award.

Entrants, students at higher education institutes in the UK, submit pencil roughs or sketches for a children's picturebook including accompanying text. Finished artwork for at least four double-page spreads is also required. Submissions are judged on the quality of illustration, looking at how pictures match with the accompanying text and showcasing an understanding and ability to reflect narrative, pacing and characterisation through illustration.

A first, second and third prize are awarded and Macmillan has the option to publish any of the prize winners.

Notable winners include:

Sara Fanelli

Jane Simmons

Lucy Cousins

Catherine Rayner

Emily Gravett.

The Klaus Flugge Prize

This award was established to recognise the most promising and exciting new picturebook illustrator and was named after Klaus Flugge, founder of Andersen Press and a long-time champion and supporter of illustration. The award is independently funded by Klaus Flugge. Inaugurated in 2016, it offers an excellent opportunity to keep abreast of new illustration talent.

Process

To form the judging panel the award seeks to involve an established illustrator, the winner from the previous year, an expert from the world of illustration and an expert from a related field – either a bookseller, librarian or reviewer. Acclaimed UK critic and reviewer Julia Eccleshare Chairs the judging panel.

The Prize is for new illustrators only; the illustrator may have created book covers or illustrations for other media or illustrated books in another genre, but can only be considered for the Prize for their first picturebook for children.

The award defines a picturebook as being for children and one in which the illustrations are as or more important than the words in telling the story; a book with illustrations on every page or on one of every pair of facing pages.

The book should have been published on a children's list in the UK between 1 January and 31 December of the respective year. Books published in another country must have been co-published in the UK within three months of the original publication date. The book must have an editor. Books that are only available in e-format, are self-published or where authors have contributed or paid for publication cannot be considered.

The Managing Director of Andersen Press, Mark Hendle (2016) commented on the establishment of the award: 'Klaus is legendary for his ability to discover, grow and nurture new talent, and has launched the careers of many of today's most distinguished illustrators. So in Andersen Press's 40th anniversary year, I think it is wonderful and fitting that Klaus decided to establish a prize that recognises and celebrates exciting new talent in children's illustrated books.'

Winners 2016–19:

Nicholas John Frith, *Hector and Hummingbird*

Francesca Sanna, *The Journey*

Kate Milner, *My Name is Not Refugee*

Jessica Love, *Julian is a Mermaid.*

The Excelsior Award

The Excelsior Award, initially known as the Stan Lee Excelsior Award, was founded in 2011 – to recognise graphic novels and manga. It is run in Sheffield and has grown to become the only nationwide book award for graphic novels and manga. It was inspired by Stan Lee, who was the co-creator of Spider-Man, X-Men and numerous comic book heroes, and instrumental to the success of Marvel Comics.

The aim of the scheme is to encourage reading for pleasure and to raise the profile of graphic novels and manga both among young people and librarians and teachers. The award currently reaches in excess of 200 schools in and beyond the United Kingdom. Dave Gibbons, artist for *2000 AD* and *Watchmen* says of the award, 'the Excelsior Award is not hype. It's a genuine effort by UK school librarians to get comics into schools. We all win!' (www.excelsioraward.co.uk/endorsement).

Process

The judging panel is formed of representatives of comic book creators, school librarians, library suppliers, booksellers and other experts. The judges draw up four shortlists: the Excelsior White is for students age 9 and above, Excelsior Blue for students aged 11 and above, Excelsior Red for students aged 14 and above and the Excelsior Black which is for students aged from 16. Each shortlist consists of five graphic novel and manga titles.

Participating schools and groups are able to register in the Autumn of the academic year if they wish to take part in judging. To participate each school or group must buy at least one set of the shortlisted books in the category that they wish to judge. This assists in providing school and public libraries with carefully selected and curated collections of an often under-resourced area of provision. Children and young people (11–18) are invited to rate each book after they have read them. Approximately ten weeks are allocated for this. Following reading, rating takes place using special forms that have been created to be easy, simple and quick to complete.

Winning books are announced at an award ceremony in June each year and speakers and guests have included luminaries of the graphic novel world such as Bryan Talbot, Andy Diggle and Ian Churchill.

In addition to the award itself, the Excelsior also encourages engagement with the awards and reading through running 'The Nuff Said' prize, which is given for the best library display to promote the award and the 'True Believers' award for the school which returns the most rating forms.

Feedback

The scheme is well received with schools and libraries as the testimonial below shows:

> 'It was our first year with the Excelsior Award. I received very positive feedback from the students and our Comic Club gets new members every month! It was a great literacy activity too.'   (School Librarian, Dublin)

It holds appeal for readers who are less confident or keen readers and for whom traditional reading might not appeal:

> 'I've been looking for something like this and it seems perfect, especially for engaging reluctant readers or pupils who wouldn't usually join a traditional reading club.'   (School Librarian, Cumbria)

> 'The students all commented on the artwork and how that in itself drew their attention to the read.'   (School Librarian, Surrey)

There has been a clear appetite for the scheme and it has improved footfall into libraries:

'I had far more pupils interested than books allowed for. I shall be investing in more sets next year. The award also brought me into contact with pupils who are not frequent of usual library visitors. New relationships have been created!'   (School, Librarian, Birmingham)

Notable winners include:
Yana Toboso, *Black Butler: Volume One*
Tom Taylor and Chris Scalf, *Star Wars: Blood Ties*
Tom King, Mikel Janin and Clay Mann, *Batman: The War of Jokes and Riddles.*

Regional book awards

Regional book awards also provide an ideal way to stimulate children and young people to become actively involved in reading. They promote new titles and help to place these into the hands of children and young people. Regional awards also offer an opportunity to support education professionals and librarians to develop their knowledge of current books and children's reading tastes, interests and abilities.

The Sheffield Book Award runs a picturebook category. This has been running since 1989 and was first won by Martin Waddell and Barbara Firth. Six titles are shortlisted for the award. Grown from an initial six schools that participated, the scheme now reaches well over two hundred and is currently sponsored by Micro Librarian Systems.

The Coventry Inspiration Awards have been running for fourteen years. Administered by the school library service, they have proven so popular that they now have an international reach. The 4–7 year old category 'What's the Story' is solely for picturebooks. Eight books are selected for the shortlist each year. These are picked by a panel of specialist librarians and teachers and are selected to represent a broad range of styles, genres and interests whilst also being inclusive.

Services Manager for Coventry School Library and Resource Service, Isobel Powell, explains, 'We include picture fiction and graphic novels in some of our categories for older students as I am a big believer in the use of pictures for all age groups, especially to help engage more reluctant and less able readers to enjoy the reading experience.'

Recognition as to the importance of picturebooks and chapter books in children's development feels to be burgeoning, as can be shown by Lancashire School Library Service who, after fifteen years of running a key stage two primary school book award to encourage reading for pleasure, have developed a sister initiative, the Brilliant Book Awards aimed at key stage one. The intention is that this award will be run in school classes and will operate as a book group encouraging reading for pleasure. The inaugural scheme launched in November 2019 and over 100 schools signed up to participate. Schools will each receive two copies of four recently published titles and children will be encouraged to read these in a relaxed and low-pressure way.

Local book awards can give early experiences of democracy in practice, encourage social, creative and critical responses to a wide range of books and encourage wider reading from a range of different sources.

International awards

International awards can provide insight into the creative and publishing output of other countries and can broaden collections and the scope of individual reading. There are too many to be able to reference individually, but to name a few: the New Zealand Book Awards for Children and Young Adults with Picture Book and Illustration categories, the Marilyn Baillie Picture Book Award run by the Canadian Children's Book Centre, the Eisner Awards for American comic books with its categories for best publication for early readers, kids and teens; and many, many more which showcase just what a rich and varied landscape illustrated books and comics constitute.

The Biennial of Illustration, Bratislava

The Biennial of Illustration Bratislava is one of the oldest and most highly regarded international honours for children's book illustration. It was first awarded in 1967 to Japanese illustrator Yasuo Segawa. The award is international in focus and is administered by the International Book Board for Young People and UNESCO. Artists are selected for the award by an international jury and an exhibition of original artwork is held in Bratislava, Slovakia. There are 11 awards comprising five Golden Apple awards, five Plaques and an overall Grand Prix winner.

Notable Grand Prix winners include:

Laura Carlin, UK, 2015

Eunyoung Cho, South Korea, 2011

Andrzej Strumillo, Poland, 1971.

The Bologna Ragazzi Award

The Bologna Ragazzi award was established in 1966 and holds considerable prestige among the industry as part of the Bologna Children's Book Fair (*La fiera del libro per ragazzi*). The fair is held annually in Spring in Bologna and is the leading professional fair for children's books and a key date for securing the selling rights. The awards honour the best production in terms of graphic and editorial qualities. The award includes the Opera Prima, an award that recognises debut authors and illustrators. A New Horizons award is given to a particularly innovative book, which the jury feels opens new horizons for the industry.

The award is judged by a panel made up of international experts and there are thousands of books nominated each year. One of the outcomes of winning is the profile that is received at the Book Fair itself and the heightened opportunity this presents for rights deals.

In addition to the awards, there is an illustrator's exhibition, which presents works of illustrators selected by a panel comprising of five experts, including publishers, illustrators or teachers of illustration. The exhibition generates considerable global interest.

The Caldecott Medal

The Caldecott Medal is awarded annually to recognise the most distinguished American picturebooks for children. The award is named after Randolph Caldecott (1846–86), an illustrator born in Chester, England. His work was influenced by Gillray and Hogarth. Caldecott was discovered by publisher Edmund Evans, who commissioned Caldecott to illustrate numerous picturebooks including, *The House that Jack Built*, *The Babes in the Wood* and various nursery rhymes.

The Caldecott Medal was first awarded in 1938 to Dorothy P Lathrop for *Animals of the Bible*. The judges also confer honours upon titles they agree are particularly noteworthy. Marcia Brown and David Wiesner jointly hold the most Caldecott Medal wins with three each while Marcia Brown holds the record for the highest number of Medal and Honour wins with a total of nine.

The Caldecott Medal recognises picturebooks for children, defined as providing the child with 'a visual experience' through 'a collective unity of story-line, theme, or concept, developed through the series of pictures of which the book is comprised'. It was established to acknowledge the artists who were felt to be equally as deserving of recognition as authors of children's books, who had been celebrated by the Newbery Medal since 1922.

Process

Artists of books nominated for the award must either be residing in the US or a citizen of the country. Illustrations must be original to the book, which must have been published first or simultaneously in the US in English in the preceding year. The book must be self-contained, not dependent on other media (i.e. sound, film, etc.) for its enjoyment.

The judging panel consists of 15 members of the Association for Library Services to Children (ALSC). Publishers can send copies of eligible books to the committee for consideration and the Chair asks the panel to identify what they believe to be strong contenders each month. In the Autumn, judges may formally nominate up to seven books and from this list of nominated titles the winner and honour books are selected. The winners are announced in January each year.

Notable winners include:

Marcia Brown, who has won the medal three times and has been honoured six times.

David Wiesner, who has won the award three times and has been honoured three times,

Maurice Sendak, who only won the award once, but received seven honours, the highest number of nominations by any illustrator to date.

In conversation with David Wiesner (2019), he reflects on the significance of the Caldecott Medal to picturebook illustrators:

A good artist uses all their skill to make the visual reading experience as rich as it can be. They are not just illustrating what it says in the text, they are adding new story elements and highlighting emotions or action only hinted at by the words. Picture books are where children first see art. It should be the best possible art. Composition, drawing, line, color, and media all affect the meaning of the story. I wouldn't approach this work with any less commitment than I would in art made for an adult audience.

The Caldecott began as a way to showcase beautifully created books. It gets children, parents, teachers and librarians talking seriously about what makes a picturebook work. It helps people see that the art is more than pretty pictures; it is part of the text.

Winning the Caldecott Medal brings great visibility to an artist's book. That is a very nice thing – this can be a hard business in which to make a living. It has been extremely gratifying for me to see my work in the midst of the long history of remarkable books that have won the Caldecott Medal.

The Children's Book Council of Australia Book of the Year Awards

The Book of the Year Awards are organised by the Children's Book Council of Australia (CBCA), a national organisation championing children's books and reading. The awards are categorised to recognise books for older readers, younger readers, early childhood picturebooks and information books. The Children's Book of the Year Award in the Picture Book category was first awarded in 1956 to Peggy Barnard. The award is made to 'outstanding books of the Picture Book genre in which the author and illustrator achieve artistic and literary unity, or in wordless picturebooks, where the story, theme or concept is unified through illustrations.' The age range for the category is 0–18, recognising the broad span of interest and appeal that picturebooks can have.

The CBCA also run the CBCA Award for a New Illustrator. Initially this was funded through the Victoria Branch of the CBCA from a legacy that was left by Mr Wallace Raymond Crichton (until 2019 the award was named 'The Crichton Award for Children's Book Illustration'). The award was first given in 1988 to Raymond Meeks. The age range for this category is also 0–18 and this award aims to recognise and grow illustrative talent.

The awards have a foundation that was created to secure funding with the aim being to aid sustainability and secure the future of the scheme.

Process
Books are nominated by publishers who must complete an official entry form, pay a submission fee (used to help fund the running of the awards) and provide the required number of copies of each nominated book.

To be eligible, books must have been published in Australia between 1 January and 31 December of the respective year. Books must also be available for purchase by the general public in Australia. Books must be written in the English language or can be dual language provided one language is English. The awards are only for books in printed format. The creator must either be an Australian citizen (regardless of where resident) or else a person resident in Australia for at least two years prior to 31

December in the year of publication, or a person who holds permanent residency status for Australia.

The judging panel for the awards as a whole consists of 15 members with three judges comprising the panel for each category. Judges include experts on literacy, visual literacy, children's literature and librarians. The appointment of judges is via application.

Notable winners include:

Bob Graham, who has won the award five times.

Shaun Tan, who has won the award four times.

Ron Brooks, who has won the award four times.

Freya Blackwood (2019), illustrator of the 2015 winner *My Two Blankets*, written by Irena Kobald, talks about the impact of winning the award:

> *My Two Blankets* received good reviews but didn't really take off until the CBCA Picture Book award was given. It was then picked up throughout the country in schools, was included in a package in the state of Victoria for all prep aged students, translated into 20 or so languages, with some bilingual editions including three fabulous bilingual editions in Australia through the ASRC. It's an interesting book though, because although it needs strong illustrations, and I feel very strongly about the message, I was really just the conduit, a means to get the story out into the world. And the author is most definitely the primary creator. It's her story. But I have always felt incredibly proud of my involvement and what I could provide for the author and her story. The fact the book won the award most definitely put it into so many more schools and hands and minds. The award is presented during Book Week here and school children around the country are encouraged to read all the shortlisted books and take an interest in the announcement of the winners.
>
> This particular award feels important to me personally because it's an award I was familiar with as a child, and although the decisions made by the judging panel can draw criticism from the book community, it is still one of the most important awards in Australian children's book publishing. I feel this book really did deserve to win it.

The Little Hakka Award

A relative newcomer, the Little Hakka Award has been running for three years and is judged and announced in Gangkeng Hakka town in Shenzhen,

China. The town itself is jointly a historic one, as the home of the Hakka people, it is a site that seeks to preserve their culture and heritage, and is also a conservation area dedicated to farming practices.

Parts of the architecture of Gangkeng Hakka town have been informed by picturebooks about the Hakka culture. Large figures feature throughout the town and characters are shown wearing traditional Hakka style hats, which were designed to keep the sun from the eyes of agricultural workers. These are now an integral part of visuals for the characters and the town offers a valuable insight into the ways that visual imagery can help to preserve cultural heritage, making this accessible to future generations.

Process
The awards themselves have several categories:

(A) Professional Group
(A1) Published
     Submissions can be made by publishers, corporations or
     individuals.
(A2) Unpublished
     Submissions can be made by corporations or individuals and
     should not be published, both complete and incomplete stories
     can be considered.
(A3) Digital
     Submissions can be made by publishers, corporations or
     individuals. This sub-category is to recognise entries that create
     stories for children with apps or networks and that use illus-
     tration as part of interactive media for children. The product
     needs to be designed for children aged between 2 and 15 years.
(B) Children's Group
     Entries for this category are by children aged between 4 and 14
     years old. Complete and incomplete stories are acceptable and
     submissions can be made by children, parents or by educational
     institutions. This category is interesting in that it showcases
     illustration as a viable profession.
(C) Little Hakka Theme Group
     Submissions can be made by publishers, corporations or
     individuals. This category takes Little Hakka as a creative entity
     and can draw upon other characters from the intellectual

property of the books:
Hakka – a six year old, wearing a traditional Hakka Summer
hat. She is the successor of the magic hat and is the lead
character in the series.

Figure 6.1 *Little Hakka Picturebook characters featured in Gangkeng Hakka
Town including bespoke shelving, full size figurines and illustration
gallery.* Photographs © Jake Hope, 2019

AMei – a happy angel who loves to lead visitors through the town

Dangdang Dog – a brave, loyal dog who follows AMei.

Liangliang Cat – a mischievous feline who often causes trouble.

Entries must be unpublished and feature an original story with a clear plot and positive content.

The modern picturebook form is relatively new in China and the awards are a useful means for helping to establish and embed a culture of creation. Winning artwork is exhibited in the town's gallery (as pictured in Figure 6.1). The town also has a picturebook library that has been devised around the characters of the original book series.

The Children's Laureate

The position of Children's Laureate has been conferred upon several illustrators since it was first instigated, with the first post held by Quentin Blake. It seeks to celebrate writers and illustrators of children's books who have demonstrated outstanding achievement in their field. The position allows post holders to champion particular projects and initiatives that they are passionate about, usually addressing particular needs facing the children's book industry. Every illustrator who has been laureate has championed the value of visual literacy and illustration. Laureates are in post for a tenure lasting two years. The laureate post grew out of discussions between author Michael Morpurgo and Poet Laureate Ted Hughes. Since its inauguration in the UK in 1999, several other countries have established similar programmes of ambassadorial roles including Australia, Ireland, Sweden, the United States and Wales.

Quentin Blake 1999–2001

Quentin was the first Laureate; he worked on two exhibitions: *Tell Me a Picture* at the National Gallery and *A Baker's Dozen* at the Bury St Edmunds Art Gallery. The *Tell Me a Picture* exhibition was formed of 26 paintings and drawings from the National Gallery's archive, selected by Quentin with one artist chosen for each letter of the alphabet. The exhibition also saw Quentin 'drawing on the walls of the gallery', the first time this had been allowed. These drawings featured characters that were designed to draw the audience to the central picture. The aim was to highlight the artistic worth of illustration and to show the role that great illustration can play in acting as a route into better appreciation for great paintings. Seminal picturebook illustrators like John Burningham and Emma Chichester Clark were hung alongside artists like Frabcusci de Goya and Paula Rego. An accompanying book, *Tell Me a Picture: Adventures in Looking at Art* was published by Frances Lincoln. Over 240,000 visitors saw the exhibition.

Quentin Blake (2019) reflects on his experience of the power of stories in pictures to reach new audiences and welcome young people into the world of reading:

> Stories in pictures, whether explicit or implied, can be wonderful, and they lead us into a special art. It's something I have written about, not least for the exhibition *Tell Me A Picture* which I organised at the National Gallery with Ghislaine Kenyon. In it, the pictures were arranged alphabetically whether by old or new masters or contemporary illustrators, and each of them offered a story. I hope and believe that many people came to the show who would not normally go to such a gallery; at any rate they queued up the front steps and the wardens were rather surprised to hear them happily laughing and talking to each other.
>
> Two other, smaller, examples. One, witnessing a little girl, who had not yet learnt to read, 'reading' *Mister Magnolia* to herself. The other for me is eloquent and comes from a conversation I had with a young photographer some years ago. He said: 'My daughter could read and write at four, before she went to school. Largely thanks to you.'

The second exhibition, *A Baker's Dozen*, was held in Bury St Edmunds Art Gallery and featured children's book illustrations, including roughs, sketches and finished artwork. It drew attention to the processes and techniques each of the featured illustrators used. The exhibition comprised of 12 illustrators plus Quentin himself making number 13 of the Baker's dozen. Chris Riddell was one of the featured illustrators and would later become Laureate himself. This was an invaluable way to raise the profile, quality and range of illustrator talent in the UK.

As a legacy of his time as Laureate, Quentin founded the House of Illustration, an idea he and colleagues conceived of as a gallery built around his archive and that of other artists. The House of Illustration opened in 2014 and is the only public gallery in the UK dedicated to illustration and graphic art.

Quentin is a patron of the Campaign for Drawing, a campaign to highlight the importance of drawing for children and adults. He led a team of artists to do a big drawing for the launch of 'The Big Draw', the world's largest drawing festival, in September 2000 where they worked on a picture for the walls of the tunnel between South Kensington Tube Station and the Museums.

The Big Draw, formerly the Campaign for Drawing, was founded in 2000 and is an arts education charity promoting visual literacy and the role that drawing can play as a tool for learning, communication and as a vessel for the imagination. The Big Draw Festival is the world's biggest celebration of drawing and takes place throughout October with events and activities happening across the world. Quentin Blake, Patron of The Big Draw commented on the power of drawing: 'We live in a verbal culture where we think words are important and drawing is merely decorative. But there are hundreds of things for which drawing is wonderfully economical and efficient. It's much easier for most of us to draw the way a deckchair works than to explain it in words.'

Anthony Browne 2009–11

A key element of Anthony Browne's work is the referential way in which works of high art feed into stories and artwork, something which helped to inform the time he spent working with the Tate Britain as their writer and illustrator in 2001–02. Anthony is one of few British recipients of the Hans Christian Andersen prize, the highest international recognition given to an author and an illustrator of children's books and recognising 'a lasting contribution to children's literature.'

Anthony's major campaign as Laureate was 'Play the Shape Game', this was based on a game he and his brother played as children where one of them would create a shape by taking a line for a walk and the other would use this as the base to make a picture. The game was used to draw attention to children's creativity seeking to demystify what it means to be an author or illustrator and raise children's aspirations in this field. Anthony created a shape which he asked celebrities to use to join him in playing the 'Shape Game'. The results were published in a book and the original artwork was auctioned to raise money for the Rainbow Trust, a charity supporting the families of children with life threatening or terminal illnesses.

Anthony also supported 'The Picture Book Project' a partnership between Action for Children and Seven Stories which highlighted the importance of picturebooks for children and the roles they provide in sharing, talking, listening and having fun. Anthony was involved in the Best New Illustrators Award with BookTrust which sought to recognise ten emerging illustrators whose work showed creative flair, artistic skill and imagination. Seven Stories curated an exhibition of Anthony's work in March 2011, *Through the Magic Mirror*. This toured numerous venues including Leeds City Museum where over 180,000 people saw it, including many visitors that had not previously visited the museum, showing the power and reach of the Children's Laureate initiative.

In Lancashire, a number of people were asked to play the shape game using a simplified outline of the map of the county. This was used as an activity for The Big Draw and a number of pieces of artwork were displayed as part of an exhibition in the Museum of Lancashire with an online collection of books from libraries supporting this.

Anthony Browne (2019) provides an insight into how he became an illustrator and what inspires his work:

> I have always loved telling stories through pictures – I've kept some of my early childhood drawings and they all contain jokes, speech bubbles and snippets of descriptive writing. It wasn't until I was 28 that I decided to try and make a career out of it. I love the combination of words and pictures, seeing the book take shape. Often the pictures can illustrate different aspects of the story that the words don't tell.
>
> When I make a picture book it's nearly always loosely autobiographical so the illustrations often refer to my life and interests. When children ask me 'where do you get your ideas from?' I usually say from everywhere – my own childhood, things my children told me, stories I've read, films I've watched and paintings I've seen. Over a period of time I have found that I was able to use images in the background to tell part of the stories that weren't in the text – like clues to what is really going on in a character's emotional and mental state.

Chris Riddell 2015–17

Chris Riddell's tenure as Children's Laureate had five focal points:

1 The Laureate Log – this was an online platform where Chris posted online drawings visually charting his involvement as the Laureate.

2 Words need Pictures – the creation of visual resources for schools, libraries and classrooms showing the value of visual literacy.
3 The Joy of Sketchbooks – working to promote daily doodling.
4 Stay Calm and Keep Reading – a celebration of school libraries and reading for pleasure.
5 The Doodler – appearance of a mysterious masked figure drawing on walls and live drawing at numerous locations and events.

In addition to the above, Chris sought to nurture, support and endorse new illustrator talent and gave workshops on illustration at Bologna, Brighton Art School and Hull School of Art and Design.

The passion Chris showed for doodling, perhaps grew out of his own interest in childhood drawing as expressed in an interview for *ACHUKA* (2007): 'I can't remember a time when I didn't draw. My older brother and I would spend hours drawing battles on paper and later, as an eight to nine year-old, I used to write and illustrate miniature newspapers full of lurid headlines.'

Chris was incredibly active on social media during his tenure helping to show the importance of visual media in digital daily life and the ability it holds to create momentum and critical mass. The #ChildrensLaureate hashtag reached over 20 million people during his time as Laureate.

The visibility and profile Chris brought to the Laureate role inspired many children and young people. At Trinity St Michael's School in Croston, they organised a trip to see Chris Riddell during his World Book Day appearance and did a programme of work building their own imaginary town map, having doodle-off challenges at lunch times and exploring other illustrators work. This was followed by a multi-school event attended by Chris during his Laureate tour of the North. As a small rural school, this was a major coup and saw Trinity St Michael's working with neighbouring secondary school, Brownedge St Mary's to make this opportunity available widely.

Lauren Child 2017–19

Lauren Child's time as Laureate focused on seeking to change attitudes and awareness of the importance of children's imagination and creativity among policy makers and gatekeepers. Her major campaign as Laureate was 'Staring into Space' which aimed to encourage children to think creatively. Lauren worked with art teacher Josey Scullard to create resources for primary school-aged children to show how children's picturebooks can be used as a stimulus for creativity. Lauren has created www.staringintospace.me to motivate people to take time out to explore and imagine the world around them.

Additionally Lauren worked with the British Council to curate the exhibition, *Drawing Words*. This celebrates ten illustrators whose work has made a significant and unique contribution to contemporary British picture book illustration. The exhibition is touring internationally creating a major showcase. Lauren also launched the Lauren Child Illustration Award in conjunction with the Betjeman Poetry Prize and House of Illustration to show the role illustrations can play in accompanying poetry. Young illustrators aged between 18 and 25 were able to illustrate prize-winning poems and an exhibition of winning work was displayed at St Pancras International Station in November 2018.

Lauren was also the illustrator of the day at trade fair the London Book Fair and delivered the BookTrust Annual Lecture in October 2017, helping to bring attention to illustration across the industry.

Cressida Cowell 2019–21

At the time of writing, Cressida Cowell has been announced as the Laureate. Both an author and an illustrator, Cressida created the highly acclaimed *How to Train your Dragon* book series which have successfully crossed into blockbuster films with Dreamworks studio. As Children's Laureate, Cressida has already created an ambitious ten-point charter, declaring:

Every child has the right to:

1   Read for the joy of it
2   Access NEW books in school libraries and bookshops
3   Have advice from a trained librarian or bookseller
4   Own their OWN book
5   See themselves reflected in a book
6   Be read aloud to
7   Have some choice in what they read
8   Be creative for at least fifteen minutes a week
9   See an author event at least ONCE
10 Have a planet to read on.

Visual literacy intersects many of these areas and with Cressida's aptitude for both visual and pictorial narratives, it is exciting to think what her tenure will bring! Cressida describes below the importance of visual awareness:

> When I was growing up, there was no internet, limited television channels, no playstation. Now the telly is glorious and incessant, children can access movies and games at the touch of a button, and they are magically 'beamed' into children's heads without them having to do anything, whereas books can only be accessed by a laborious act of decoding. Even if a child doesn't have a learning difficulty, books can come to be associated with school and hard work, but if a child has dyslexia, it can be worse than that. In that case, books can sometimes come to represent something that actively makes the child feel stupid, and how on earth can you love something that makes you feel stupid?
>
> Which is why it is so important that children are allowed to read picture books beyond the age people think they 'should' be read. Pictures can be accessed without any 'decoding', so even when the child is struggling with deciphering the letters, they can be enjoying the story through the pictures. Pictures in themselves can also help the decoding process. Cartoon strips such as Calvin and Hobbes, for example, use sophisticated language that the child is better able to absorb because they are being given clues as to the meaning through the pictures.
>
> Children of today are, if anything, even more visual than previous generations, because of their exposure to the screen. So it makes sense to use that visual awareness to help them learn, not just the mechanics of reading, but the joy of it. Books are transformative magic, and that magic should be available to everyone.

In the UK around 10,000 children's books are published annually. Awards can play a valuable role in helping to navigate through this high number of books, highlighting some of the most innovative creations and creators and offering a snapshot into the development of the field. High profile positions, like the Children's Laureate initiative, can draw attention to key areas in the field that need consideration or development and have helped to engender positive change and new opportunities.

CHAPTER 7

Looking to Learn: an insight into visual literacy for information

There is an increasing tendency for information to be conveyed through visual means. This is far from a new phenomenon, charts and graphs have long drawn relations between sets of statistical data; the cartographers of old created maps which conveyed the geography and topography of our landscape; and mathematicians and logisticians have used flow-charts to help to visually demonstrate sophisticated algorithms. Drawing upon this history, visuals have an increasingly important role to play in communicating information to young people and there is a growing market for high quality illustrated information books for children.

Stephen Biesty (2019), illustrator and author of the bestselling *Incredible Cross-Sections* books discusses the development of his unique style of illustrated information books:

> I went to study illustration at Brighton College of Art in 1980 where I made large freehand perspective drawings of buildings. During my second year, I discovered the historical reconstruction drawings of the artists Alan Sorrell and David Macaulay. This was an important turning point for me and I began experimenting with my first cutaways and cross-section drawings to show how castle defences worked.
>
> I started working as a freelance illustrator in 1985. Initially I thought I might work somewhere like the National Trust or English Heritage creating explanatory drawings of historic buildings, but I found this area too dry and limiting. There were many better opportunities for me in adult and children's publishing where I had some freedom of expression to try and bring subjects to life.
>
> At this early stage, I often struggled as a commercial artist because I seemed to lean naturally towards wanting to put far too much detail into my work and as a result taking far too long. However, in 1989 I had a stroke of good fortune, the detailed illustrations I had been making for Mitchell

Beazley and Octopus Books attracted the attention of Dorling Kindersley. I created a test piece for them of a cross-sectioned Ocean Liner which was a gatefold spread nearly 1m wide. Peter Kindersley told me 'Take as long as you like.'

So I now had an opportunity to develop a highly detailed labour-intensive style of illustration that included lots of people and extra content. I found I could create an overwhelmingly detailed effect by simply going over my finished pencil drawing with a waterproof rOtring pen ink line. I then built up watercolour washes over this to create a richly toned 3D effect without losing any fine detail. I finished it off by picking out the fine linework again to try and make the detail in the artwork glitter. The finished Ocean Liner illustration worked beautifully and was the beginning of the internationally bestselling *Incredible Cross-Sections* book.

Biesty received the encouraging fan letter below in 2014:

Your work has been a part of my life for over 20 years and counting. I remember long, weekly trips to the local library to trade *Castle* for *Man-Of-War*, then after a week with that, I'd pick up the *Everything* book. Me and my siblings would trade the book nightly before bed, spending hours and evenings and sometimes days pouring over every character in the pages of those books...I'm 24 now, married and have a 4 month old son...because of books like yours I've remained an ever curious individual who continues to look, learn and find new things about everything.

The power of visual information

Someone in possession of a sound ability to infer information from graphics is equipped with the power to understand content from a range of countries and cultures regardless of aptitude in the particular language spoken in these countries. This becomes a particularly important skill for international communication; consider the need for internationally recognisable road signs and comprehensible signage at airports and transport destinations where numerous travellers need to be able to understand where onward buses, trains and even toilets are located.

Graphic information is easily able to convey ideas around size and perspective, enabling readers not only to understand something, but to experience it though seeing too. Take for instance, books like *Actual Size* by Steve Jenkins, which reproduced a range of different creatures according to their actual size and made use of different page layouts, elements of the creatures and page pull-outs in the book to create a realistic likeness of the size of the creatures. Describing how the idea for the book came about Steve (2019) states:

> I was at the San Diego zoo with my older son Alec, who was 12 at the time. We were outside the gorilla paddock and noticed a life-size metal cast of a gorilla's hand. Most of the adults who passed by (and every child) held their hand up and compared it to the gorillas. That cartoon light bulb over my head lit up, and I thought 'this is a perfect children's book concept.' Well, maybe I didn't think 'perfect.' But viable, for sure.

See Figure 7.1 for an example of a crocodile in Steve's book *Actual Size*.

Figure 7.1 *Artwork image from Actual Size by Steve Jenkins* © Houghton Mifflin Harcourt, 2004

Books can help to introduce information about our feelings, helping us better identify and understand our emotional states and experiences when very young. Eva Eland (2019) discusses the means via which illustration and images can carry such information and the visual language she draws on to achieve this in her book, *When Sadness Comes to Call*:

> Developing the book and researching the emotion of sadness, I found that there are many aspects of this emotion and the challenge was to incorporate some of the more layered meanings, without losing the simplicity and openness the text and images provide. The tools I have used to achieve this are a limited colour palette, composition, use of visual metaphors, body language and the build-up of tension in the sequence.

In my illustration practice, I have discovered the narrative power of archetypal images and visual metaphors and how they can convey a lot of information (which is extremely useful for me as an illustrator, even though I run the risk of using clichés). An example of the use of this would be the suitcase that the personification of Sadness carries, when it 'arrives unexpectedly' in the book. It indicates that Sadness is a visitor, yet we are unsure of how long it might stay. And even though it might not be interpreted as such by every reader, it can also allude to the emotional baggage we tend to carry around in life and the possibility of letting go of some of that luggage that can weigh us down occasionally.

The power of visual signifiers such as those Eva describes, can help young readers to learn and understand their emotions. Pictures are an important tool to aid learning and to convey complex information; they stimulate readers to respond directly to what is experienced through sight and can help people access and experience the wonders of the wider world. There is great value, therefore, in the production of high-end information titles. Debbie Foy (2019), publishing director for Wren & Rook discusses the developing market for such titles:

> The rise of high-end factual storytelling has changed the landscape of children's non-fiction publishing. Children are sophisticated visual consumers. They are bombarded daily with visual information on their smartphones: adverts, gifs, memes, brands and insta-ready content. Illustration and graphics-wise, it's vital that we are speaking *to* the child, not *about* them. Many non-fiction books appeal aesthetically more to the purchaser than the end-user – so we go all out to commission a diverse range of innovative, intriguing and aspirational illustrators, with playfulness, energy and spirit. Our ultimate aim is to transport children into new worlds of discovery.

In the digital age when information is recorded and retrieved with rapidity, visual means are an easy way to convey complex information quickly and accessibly.

Displaying information through visual means

Charts and graphs
These can be used for showing the relationship between statistical data in an easily accessible visual form. Flowcharts can show interrelations and work-patterns to achieve a complex task.

Maps
Useful for showing the geographic layout and topography of an area of space or an urban centre. These help readers to orientate their position and to navigate around unfamiliar landscapes identifying key features.

Infographics
A collection of images with minimal text allowing an overview of a topic or subject area.

Memes
A term first used by Richard Dawkins in his book *The Selfish Gene* – used to describe a unit capable of carrying cultural ideas, symbols and practice that can be transmitted from one mind to another.

Word Clouds
Word clouds, or tag clouds, are a useful way of grouping key words pertaining to a particular subject and showing the importance or prominence of individual words through their relative size. Word clouds can be grouped in particular shapes and can be used as an accessible way of displaying information such as the most borrowed item from the library collection, the most popular themes or subjects.

Photography
Photographs can provide primary source material to convey news and give the appearance of an objective viewpoint on numerous subjects – sciences, arts, technologies, history. Find out more from artist, Ifeoma Onyefulu, on page 134.

Illustrations
There are a huge range of styles of illustration which can give radically different reading experiences when encountering information. Stephen Biesty, see pages 129–30, discussed his meticulously detailed, accurate cross-sections books. The comic book format can also be a great conduit for

communicating information in an appealing and engaging form as illustrator and graphic novelist Gene Luen Yang comments, 'Students today are inundated with information. That information can come as words or it can come as pictures. Students must be able to decipher both, and the comics medium is the perfect way to teach them how.'

Ifeoma Onyefulu (2019) is a photographer and author; she created the alphabet information book, *A is for Africa*. Here, she discusses the appeal of photography and how and why she uses it in her books:

If you've ever been told a story by a great storyteller, you want to bottle up the feelings of warmth you've experienced forever. So I try to create in my books that warm feeling I felt as a child when my mother and grandfather, both great storytellers, used to tell me stories. Photography also captures a moment and preserves it, and I feel photographs are easier for children to use for learning about other cultures. As my books are set in Africa, a continent that is still not fully understood by many people elsewhere, I feel photography will have more of an impact on my readers.

Children will relate to the photographs easily. The images encourage discussions and questions within a setting, for example my book *Deron Goes to Nursery School* will help children learn about other children, about similarities and differences.

When I have an idea for a story, I write it down and then I do rough drawings of what I wish to photograph and research the best place (the best African country) to get the photographs, and afterwards select pictures that will best illustrate the story.

I feel photography is the best medium for the kind of books I write. I also use it because I used to be a freelance photographer for a local newspaper. A good photograph captures the right moment with good intention. Photography helps to counteract stereotypes and introduce children to other cultures. It encourages discussions about how other people live. In my view it brings the world closer to my readers.

Finding fun in learning

It should not be forgotten that there can be a place for humour in visual information texts too. Indeed, use of the comic medium can make learning feel fun, playful and less like a chore. Here illustrator and cartoonist Adam Murphy (2019) discusses his popular *Corpse Talk* book series which began life as a strip in *The Phoenix* comic. Adam uses a TV chat show format, where he is the host, to interview various dead historical figures in a fun and engaging way:

> The TV chat show format has been remarkably fruitful for doing history for kids, as it allows for so many different approaches to each subject. I can ask a dumb question, to allow an interviewee to explain something I need to be sure kids know. I can ask a modern question the historical person might not know about, but that makes things relevant for a modern readership. And I can challenge conventional narratives by raising difficult or embarrassing facts the interviewees might prefer remain consigned to history. Plus of course, as the interviewer, my own stupidity, excessive enthusiasm or snarky one-liners give lots of ways to insert jokes, which helps keep readers engaged, and cements facts in their memories.

It is easy to dismiss certain types of reading because it does not adhere to the constraints and delineations of an established canon, however there is value to be gained from reading in all types of formats. There has been a tendency to devalue reading and learning through visual information, that is accessed via apps or games. A popular game relying upon visual subject groups is Top Trumps – a card game where numerical information about a particular subject area, e.g. cars, cats, characters from Star Wars, are pitted against one another. With short descriptions, or biographies, about each entry and a list of facts, the cards encourage learning through comparison and game play. Top Trumps were first published in 1978 and have stimulated learning through play for more than 40 years. The Top Trumps games can also lead young people into new reading and subject areas with packs being sold based on a variety of topics including Doctor Who, Roald Dahl, Marvel comic characters and the like. An enjoyable activity for reading groups can be creating a similar card game of their own, perhaps using book heroes, or through researching a particular subject area. The power of games to stimulate learning through play and develop reading for pleasure should not be underestimated.

Many libraries have set up Lego clubs as a means for children to play and learn through use of the popular construction toy. It can be a useful way to introduce children and young people to the skill of following visual instructions, progressing through complicated design tasks to complete a

Lego build. Timed challenges, competitions to build or to complete their own designs and create instructions for building these all equip children with valuable skills, teaching them to follow instructions and compose their own by breaking the tasks down into manageable stages. As part of the 2019 National Libraries Week campaign, CILIP ran a competition to design and build the library of the future out of Lego. Hundreds of children and young people engaged with the competition creating innovative and imaginative libraries out of Lego bricks, showing the versatility and creative capacity of the form in communicating ideas and imagination.

Creating visually rich learning environments

Visual literacy can be embedded across learning environments to help to enhance and enrich the experiences children and young people have. This section will explore some of the ways in which this can be achieved and the means through which it can support learners.

Visual note taking

Not only do children and young people learn through reading visual information, illustrative and pictorial representations can be used to help create notes or stories, allowing children to record and retain information that they have accessed. One way this might be achieved in practice is through visual minutes – capturing and visualising ideas in a dynamic way in the sequence in which they occur. When working for Lancashire libraries, visual note taking was used to help record different types of prejudice that young people felt the community had experienced through history and created a visual resource leading from the past to outlining the group's hopes and ambitions for the future. This method results in a clear and memorable visual resource that can be displayed after the event for reference or as an interest or focal point. Visual minutes might use different colours, shapes, fonts and images to help capture the messages and ideas. They are also an effective way of recording a timeline of events and conversations as they happen and as details unfold.

The School Library Service (SLS)

School library services traditionally provide collections of books to match curriculum needs. Learning can be supported visually and kinaesthetically through object provision. Kirklees Booksplus offer a service providing curriculum support boxes that include books and objects designed to enhance young peoples' learning experience; they are cross-curricular and key stage appropriate. The boxes contain a broad and inclusive range of books (usually around 20 titles including a mix of information titles and fiction) that are collected together with a range of relevant objects or artefacts (usually around five). These are accompanied by other audio-visual resources (DVDs, audio titles, musical instruments), where available. The service also offered a fabric library, which documents the textile industry of the area.

Staff member, Alison Brumwell (2019), developed multi-sensory resources to support the teaching of philosophy for children (P4C). This included guidance notes, session plans, themed objects, games and a class set of picturebooks, with the idea being that resources could be used to create a centre of discovery and enquiry within the classroom. Whilst a wealth of downloadable online materials exists for teachers, the purpose of the boxes was to provide a structured and focused set of resources which offered both visual and tactile stimuli. Alison explains:

> The basic offer to schools by local authorities with a schools library service (SLS) varies widely; while most have a book exchange programme and themed collections of print resources, the positive impact upon teaching and learning of using objects, artefacts and multi-sensory resources in conjunction with these is immeasurable.
>
> Teaching and learning styles vary widely too. Even fluent readers with easy access to print benefit hugely from being able to handle a 3D object. A deeper, richer understanding of basic concepts, including shape, pattern, colour and scale, is possible for younger children and emergent readers and allows those with learning difficulties or sensory loss to participate more fully in the learning experience. Teachers can augment and enliven their schemes of work and lesson plans for older learners; whether it's linking to a basic unit of the curriculum (like the First World War) or developing a community of enquiry within the classroom. Local history and mapping is a key area which can be developed through a creative use of objects, artefacts and ephemera.

An example of the kind of artefacts which Alison describes is Fenella the tiger, which inspired the creation of a learning programme that has fed into further creative work as Alison details below:

Fenella the tiger is an excellent example of a local history project that involved partnership working between public libraries, local schools and artists and the schools library service. The story of this real-life tiger who came to tea spawned two home-grown books, an exhibition of photographs, a travelling circus train collection of resources developed by Kirklees local history librarians and a commemorative mosaic which was installed in Holmfirth Library ten years ago. What began as local folklore eventually grew to include *A Tiger's Tale*, a 2018 play by Mike Kenny. Fenella's story is a wonderful journey which spans nearly 70 years; made much more vibrant by the images and creative output which still inspire both children and adults.

Simplified Dewey

The Dewey system of classification can be difficult for children and young people to get to grips with. A simplified form using colours as a visual clue has been adopted by some school library services to help children become familiar with the system. Kirklees Booksplus uses simplified Dewey decimal classification to help aid children's navigation through information titles. The system uses a maximum of two decimal places and utilises coloured classification labels for all primary stock. The coloured labels are a simple and easy way to identify a visual system of classifying materials and retrieving titles on subjects that children are interested in or studying. Although aimed at the primary market, several secondary schools and academies have also adopted the same labelling system meaning there is ease of transition as children move up the education system. Booksplus in Kirklees and Coventry are currently the only services producing labels for school library service stock which means Booksplus sends labels out to schools across the United Kingdom. Colour coding is widely used across West Yorkshire as well as in Kirklees.

Similar colour coding, to help support children in locating subject specific information titles, is used by the School Library Service in Lancashire. Their scheme is called 'Code Cracker' and encourages children to learn to 'crack the code' of Dewey as an initial step on their journey to becoming lifelong learners. In Lancashire, trials were held in public libraries where the children's information sections were classified using this method so there was parity between the system encountered in schools and in the public library. The system uses coloured spine stickers and posters to help children become familiar with the subject areas and where particular titles or subjects are located.

Partnerships to create visual learning opportunities

Local partnerships can bring value to the library offer. Whether that be working with local schools, museums or archives, libraries can enrich their learning offer by drawing on local connections. Working in collaboration with local primary and secondary schools, for example, could provide opportunities for developing artwork displays. This could be work that children and young people have been undertaking as part of existing courses, or it may be that more in depth ways of presenting information can be explored. For example, where collections of local history materials exist children could come to the library to carry out research to discover how and why the local area has changed. This can be linked to learning outcomes with the geography and history curriculum by exploring archival photographs, posters of events and advertisements to discover the preoccupations and leisure pursuits in times past and comparing those with the present.

Working alongside museums and archives can create opportunities to use historic visual documents and photographs of artefacts as part of learning to inform children's knowledge and understanding. In Lancashire, the School Library Service and the Records Office collaborated on a project called 'Peter's Preston'. This used facsimile archival material to build a picture of the life of a real child, Peter, growing up in historic Lancashire through the use of census records, birth and death certificates, historic photographs, town maps and plans. This provided a rich insight into the locality and the experiences of children of the same age as the child learners.

A love of information or non-fiction books can drive creativity itself. Yuval Zommer (2019), illustrator of the award-winning *The Big Book* series for Thames & Hudson – which has over 50,000 copies in print and has been translated into over 20 languages – discusses his love for non-fiction:

> I have always loved non-fiction books, as a child they tapped into my curiosity about the big wide world and inspired me to learn all about subjects such as biology, geography, history and much more. So of course I was more than delighted to finally get to write and illustrate my own non-fiction books.
>
> The non-fiction titles I knew from my childhood had one school of thought that said pictures should be on one side of the double page and text

on the other. Or pictures should go on top and a text paragraph goes below.

My own approach to creating an engaging non-fiction title is to create a narrative flow throughout the book so the reading experience itself becomes a journey of discovery either across the page as in *The Big Books* series or in a long continuous concertina format as in *The Street Beneath My Feet* and *The Skies Above My Eyes*. So it's 'text in the pictures' or 'pictures in the text' for me. It is this marriage of words and images that lifts a book from just conveying information to a loved book children would want to read again and again.

Finally, one of the main reasons why I love non-fiction so much is that it allows me to combine art with science. I believe that the two not only go well together but actually belong together. My books are all about the natural world, and for me, Mother Nature is the ultimate artist and ultimate scientist. It is nature's beauty and inventiveness that really inspired my books and is currently inspiring my next one!

Yuval is a great example of how creating books that combine words and pictures to present information in a form that children wish to return to over and over again can create an appetite for learning to last a lifetime.

CHAPTER 8

A Room with a View: making the most of visual literacy in libraries and in creating reading environments

The final chapter of this book is about creating a reading environment that recognises and builds opportunities around visuals. Whether in libraries, schools or even in the home, building attractive and engaging environments where children feel excited to explore and discover helps to make reading irresistible.

With careful planning visual literacy can influence stock, services, staff and space. Throughout the course of the book we've explored the ways in which visual literacy can be used as a tool for promoting reading and developing readers. This chapter seeks to raise understanding and awareness among librarians and education practitioners of how visual literacy can be used in the library and other settings, taking into account book stock, displays and the learning environment. The chapter is divided into two parts, beginning with an overview of some of the areas of library and reading provision in which visual literacy can be applied, followed by a number of case studies to give practical guidance and inspiration for projects and activities.

Stock

Awareness of stock is the foundation for carefully curating a collection. Selection and promotion of stock is a valuable way to keep children interested and engaged in collections. Awards can provide a useful framework for promoting and recommending titles and referring back to those we explored in Chapter 6 may be useful.

As the majority of public libraries in the United Kingdom have moved from approval collections to supplier selections – a system where libraries liaise with suppliers in creating specification sheets for individual libraries, including community profiles – this has meant retaining stock knowledge and awareness of new and key titles has become more challenging for staff.

With libraries facing an increasing lack of stock knowledge, there is a valuable role for book reviews and listings in helping librarians to develop their collections. Joy Court (2019), reviews editor of the School Library Association journal, *The School Librarian*, talks about her approach to curating this valuable resource.

> *The School Librarian* is a quarterly journal reviewing in excess of 250 texts per issue and receiving approximately half as many again submitted. Reviews that do not make it into print appear on the SLA website (www.sla.org.uk) so members have access to the widest possible range of titles.
>
> I was delighted to discover I had inherited such experts in my reviews team as Jane Doonan and Prue Goodwin, and was able to add Marianne Bradnock and Professor Morag Styles, as well as several past Kate Greenaway judges to be confident that I had a pool of key reviewers to direct the best books to. The team also includes experts in graphic novels and enthusiasts for the highly illustrated informational texts that are enjoying such a renaissance in publishing now. The quality and depth of reviews is what makes us stand out.

Reviews and listings can help ensure a good knowledge of contemporary publishing output, but commercial publishing does not always represent all sectors and groups within the community. In instances where this is the case, some libraries have found that software like Photoshop and Desktop Publishing Packages together with more affordable print technologies make it possible to create stories and titles to better reflect these interests. School Librarian of the Year (2016), Amy McKay, created Corby Business Academy Books (CBA Books). Using images as the core, CBA books is able to produce books that relay the experiences of special needs students in the school in a format that is accessible and appropriate. This type of personal interaction and ownership of books can also empower children allowing them the opportunity to create and share their work. Similar schemes have been adopted in Lancashire with Gypsy, Roma and Traveller families producing books that show different types of homes, families and lifestyles mapping this against elements of the Early Years Foundation Stage curriculum and using photographs and simple text to ensure representation.

Displays

Displays are a powerful way of helping to entice children to particular books and topics. This can be as simple as creating opportunities to put books on front-on displays so that the designed front covers are on view.

Creating displays using books of one colour can be an eye-catching way of gaining attention and can contribute to association with a particular mood or season (see the section on the role of colour in this book, pages 24–7).

Displays might be organised by theme and it is possible to use thematic elements to build a display around holiday reads – for instance using buckets and spades, blues and yellows to indicate, sun, sand, sky and sea for summer. Alternatively creating displays around particular books presents opportunities to promote a particular author or series, perhaps to tie in with an author or illustrator visit, or to celebrate the books on an awards shortlist.

When Jonathan Stroud's *The Amulet of Samarkand* won the Lancashire Book of the Year Award in 2005, I created a display around the *Bartimaeus* books, using a gargoyle, ivy, lining paper coated with pebble stone textured spray paint and using lighting to create atmosphere. Quotes from the book were included on specially designed poster templates and it really drew attendees focus helping to showcase the book and the reasons why the young judges had selected this as their winner.

Windows also provide a good opportunity for visual displays and to attract interest from people that might not ordinarily visit the library. Some illustrators and designers offer window art as part of their visits. For example, as part of National Libraries Week in 2019, author Chloe Daykin, who has a background in graphic design, ran a competition to visit a library and create a forest window display to tie in with the promotion of her book *Fire Girl, Forest Boy*.

Representation can also be achieved through displays and targeted promotions. As part of a year of visual literacy in Lancashire, I explored the ways that library activity, partnerships, space and collections could be focused around the immediacy of images by organising a promotion, 'Around the World in 80 Picturebooks'. The promotion was intended as a means to highlight outstanding illustrations showcasing and originating from a range of different cultures. 80 books were selected and included titles that were first published in other countries, books in translation and books which gave insight and information into other cultures drawing upon a range of different artistic techniques and styles. Staff were encouraged to select titles from this list of 80 for storytimes and to create front-on displays and creative promotions to draw attention to a stock area that is traditionally difficult to market.

Services

Alongside the stock that libraries or reading environments hold, special activities or events can be organised to help encourage use of and greater understanding of the collection. This section will explore some of the opportunities that can be offered. These can be physical, making use of the actual resources of the collection and the space on offer, or they might be digital, using information and communication technology to devise and deliver the activity.

Artist visits

Inviting illustrators for library visits can be a powerful service addition; they generate excitement and inspiration for young people and provide a launchpad into reading for less engaged readers. The opportunity to see live illustration can be mesmeric and provides other ways of seeing and thinking about the world. To make the most of your illustrator visit, make sure the children and young people are prepared for what to expect. Giving them the opportunity to explore the background, lifestyle and influences of illustrators can help bring added value to the visit and encourage greater engagement. Ensure copies of the illustrator's books are available for sale and signing after the event, both for individual purchases and to be added to the library collection – this will create opportunities for children to learn more about the creator's work through self-discovery capitalising upon the interest and intrigue that a well-planned visit can stimulate. Festivals can also provide an excellent opportunity to introduce audiences to the work of different authors and illustrators. Case study 8.1 focuses on the Lakes International Comic Art Festival and may be of interest to readers wishing to learn more.

It is important to arrange visits from a diverse and inclusive range of artists and illustrators that inspire all children and young people. Speaking Volumes have created a new publication, *Breaking New Ground*, which highlights children's writers and illustrators of colour. This is a useful guide to aid in stock selection and indeed for selecting authors and illustrators for visits and events, helping to ensure that a diverse range of talent is included in these opportunities. The brochure provides a geographic breakdown of where individuals are based making it easy to identify those who are in close proximity thereby reducing associated travel costs. The guide is available in printed form and electronically from the Speaking Volumes website speaking-volumes.org.uk.

Book-inspired activities

Special storytime sessions are a great way to introduce new books and aid interaction with collections. These can be themed as picturebook parties or picnics. Several libraries have also arranged successful pyjama parties to help draw attention to ideal books for bedtime reads. To bring to life a series featuring the same character, you could try sourcing a character costume and putting on a guest appearance, looking at a range of titles by the same illustrator or author or focusing on a particular theme.

Character costumes can be a fun and engaging way of creating visual excitement among very young children where author and illustrator visits have little context. A range of costumes are available from providers like Rainbow Designs, although it is also possible to create outfits. These can form a great way to add value to book weeks, festivals and events and are particularly well-suited for young children who might not yet have any concept of what an author or illustrator is.

The idea of creative play can be a powerful one in enticing children to explore the layout and physical space of a library. Libraries can find inspiration in characters within books and the way that illustrators create immersive reading experiences. For example, in cartoonist Jamie Smart's *Find Chaffy* books readers are encouraged to seek out a number of friendly and fun little creatures, on the busy pages of a book. Other 'hidden' characters include Richard Scarry's Goldbug, the Usborne duck in Stephen Cartwright's titles and Colin Thompson's books even feature his dog! All of these characters encourage children to look closely, searching out detail in visually rich illustrations. This could be replicated in the library setting, for instance creating enlarged copies of pictures of the characters to encourage library hunts. As part of Lancashire's year of visual literacy, I used Jamie Smart's Chaffies as part of a creative learning opportunity made available in each of Lancashire's 70+ libraries allowing children to explore the library setting. The Youth Libraries Group are currently running a social media campaign using the Usborne duck, with the hashtag #Duckintolibraries. The idea is to publicise and market the different range of activities and links that make up the modern library offer by photographing the Usborne duck in a range of places and engaging with a broad range of library services; this has included showcasing 3D printing, accessible technologies and conferences. Larger book trails can also be created through whole towns and cities, Case study 8.4 explores a trail carried out by Wild in Art across Manchester.

Craft groups could also be encouraged to produce items which match with particular characters. As part of the Lancashire Reading Trail craft groups created knitted versions of each of the characters featured on the Reading Trail materials, even producing patterns so that other library-based knit and natter groups could replicate these. The characters also inspired songs created by the library staff.

Music and the arts

Visual literacy can open up opportunities across many areas of library collections. This could include an exploration of programmatic music; titles like Prokofiev's *Peter and the Wolf*, Saint-Saëns *Carnival of the Animals*, or Mendelssohn's *Hebrides Overture* offer opportunities to visualise elements of landscape, setting and characters and, in the case of *Peter and the Wolf*, the way stories and music can intertwine. Similarly, Adele Geras' ballet stories which focus upon classics like *Swan Lake* and *The Nutcracker*, demonstrate the evocative interplay of music with storytelling that brings to mind vivid imagery. Adele (2019) discusses her collaboration on these stories with Emma Chichester Clark:

> I remember the writing of the *Magic of the Ballet* stories with great pleasure. It was conceived from the beginning as a series that would be illustrated by Emma Chichester Clark. Laura Cecil was agent to both of us and it was she who brought us together, so to speak. I wanted it to be a little more than a simple retelling of the plots of various ballets. That's why each story has a kind of extra section which tells young readers a little of the history and traditions of this rather underrated art form. Emma's pictures lifted the books and made them beautiful.

Illustrator James Mayhew has also held concerts with orchestras while doing live painting exploring the relationship between music and the arts. A series of graphic novels offering an introduction to stories from famous operas also exists with powerful visuals conveying the narrative. Libraries could explore tying books like these with audio or audio-visual recordings for dual loans.

Photography and film

A number of illustrators and graphic novelists cite TV and film as inspiring their style and creation of visual narratives.

Edward Ross, author and illustrator of *Filmish* offers a history and different critical perspectives on films in his graphic novel. The book provides useful background that can help to inform creative projects in photography and film. Edward (2019) discusses his use of the comic form to create a heightened sense of awareness about the composition, narrative and viewer experience of film in his book, *Filmish*:

> With *Filmish* I sought to find a way to discuss the history and theory of cinema away from the walls of text I had faced at university. I loved film theory as a student, but it always mystified me why some academics felt it necessary to shroud interesting ideas in academic jargon or opaque prose. Using the comics form in *Filmish* I could work to bring interesting film theory to a wider audience, stripping away the inaccessible elements of academic discourse and replacing them with fun and attractive visuals.

Author and illustrator Chris Mould has worked on television and film creating concept art for animated projects. In an interview for *ACHUKA* (2007) he discusses the influences of film and television on his work and the ways in which visual narratives have helped to influence and inform this:

> A lot of my personal influences for my [book] worlds come from film and TV. I like all the old horror films but I also like humour. So the dark and sinister world of Royston Vasey from TV's *The League of Gentlemen* was a massive influence on me. This and films like Stephen King's *The Shining* or the original film of *The Wicker Man*. Sinister and dark but not gory. A lot of this is to do with strange isolated places and what goes on there. None of what I mention is children's viewing but I hope that what I conjure up brings something new to children's books.

Looking at the influence of TV and film can offer another route in to engaging young people, and particularly under confident readers, in books. Librarians could for instance bring together a collection of books, comics and graphic novels that draw inspiration from TV and film and encourage young people to explore and respond to these creatively. One way to approach this could be to invite young people to create book trailer based on these books. Book trailers can offer a visual insight into stories and help to promote unfamiliar books. They can also be a fun way to make creative opportunities for young people to learn new skills; these might be in filming, directing, or composing and performing incidental music, which carries mood and atmosphere. Encouraging active participation in the creation of book trailers not only forges opportunities for creativity and expression, but also helps young people to better experience and understand the makeup and mechanics of stories and how they operate. These can be created simply, without the need for specialist equipment, by using PowerPoint or Powtoons, with a mix of images – photographs or drawings – book quotes and sound files to give an accessible, reader-led means for book promotion. Digital photography can also be used as a base for local studies and more on this can be found in Case study 8.5 which looks at the Secret Slough photography project.

Digital opportunities

Visual media is becoming an increasingly important way to communicate; children and young people are able to share their mood and feelings through visual language such as gifs, emojis and memes. As the world in which children and young people are interacting becomes increasingly digital, it is important to find ways of developing the reading offer to embrace digital. Technological advancements are providing new and exciting opportunities to engage young people in visual storytelling. Readers are able to personalise content to match their needs, aesthetic tastes and values; to gamify and to create.

The National Library for Children and Young Adults in Seoul, South Korea has taken their digital reading offer to the next level. The library successfully interweaves both physical and digital images in its design and services, creating an interactive, engaging and immersive reading environment. This features exhibition space but also an interactive visual storytelling room where children and young people are able to literally enter the world of a book and become a part of the story. The interactive storytelling area was installed in 2009. The programme is targeted at children between the ages of 5 and 8 and the facility is able to accommodate up to seven children at a time. Three-dimensional virtual reality and motion recognition programmes create an immersive reading experience using a screen, projector, computer, camera and audio. The facility regularly receives over 1,500 participants annually and children express their excitement at becoming the characters in stories (see Figure 8.1). The library also offers multi-lingual stories as video files, images carrying the meaning as children encounter new or less familiar languages.

Figure 8.1 *Children interacting with the visual storytelling room at the National Library for Children and Young Adults* © National Library for Children and Young Adults, South Korea, 2019

The visual storytelling room requires specific technical equipment and a sizable budget to realise but many cost effective opportunities exist through a growing number of webs and apps. Storybird, for instance is an online platform for creating stories. It is possible to upload photographs and drawn images or to select from existing artwork on the site to create your story. You can produce comics, flash fiction or longer stories using illustration as a catalyst and to help structure the story. The site has different quizzes, challenges and prompts. Over 9 million writers in more than 100 countries around the world have used Storybird to help create stories. These can be used as activities or assignments in classes or to build on children's reading group activities. The stories can be shared by publishing these online and the site is looking at developing printing opportunities. Find out more at www.storybird.com.

The ability to interact with books via apps is a developing area in the children's book market but it is yet to be widely adopted by children's publishers in the UK. Despite initial interest in the digital processes, Nosy Crow, the pioneering children's publisher, closed their apps department in Spring 2018 due to its inability to generate revenue. The limited app production which does happen in the UK is largely by independent producers in collaboration with publishers and rights holders. For example, Kuato Studios created 'The Famous Five Adventure Game' in conjunction with Enid Blyton Entertainment. Kuato Studios describe themselves as a creative studio focusing on engaging children in narrative play for learning. 'The Famous Five Adventure Game' allows players to navigate through the settings of a mystery as they attempt to solve it, selecting a character from Blyton's quintet that they would most like to play. Kris Turvey (2017), Kuato Studios creative director, describes some of the challenges in designing the game:

> One of the biggest challenges was trying to create a game that would allow for open, free-form play and still generate a unique, compelling story on every play session. As part of our TalesMaker engine, we developed a system to both track the player's actions and weighed them for narrative interest in order to make the most compelling stories possible.

The company won the UK Literacy Association Digital Book of the Year for the game adaptation and their 'Marvel Hero Tales' has been nominated for Best Educational Game at the Tiga Games Industry Awards. This game is an innovative literacy program aimed at children aged 5–11 and featuring graphic novel characters like Captain America, Iron Man and Spider-Man. The programme allows children to shape a story through the power of language and was developed with experts in language development. Towards the close of the game, children can turn their story into their own comic book.

This development in technology allows young people to create their own stories in fun and interactive ways; by drawing on the popularity of gaming there is the potential to attract new and less confident readers. Graphic novelist, Edward Ross (2019) talks about his attempt to bring the world of gaming to a wider audience in his forthcoming graphic novel *Gamish*:

> My graphic novel *Gamish* attempts to bring the history and theory of video games to a wider audience. With this project, comic illustration has had the benefit over screen captured images by providing me a chance to create evocative and essentialised versions of a video game's imagery. Video games are a deeply experiential medium, and comics offer a chance to reflect not just the graphical reality of a game, but a sense of the idealised image that rests in the player's memory.

Space

The physical space of the library or reading environment can use visual literacy as an integral part of its design to make the space immersive and to stimulate creativity and engagement.

Design

As well as being instrumental to decisions around stock itself, a knowledge of visual literacy can also inform the design and layout of the physical library space and service resources. Visual literacy can build immersive environments that are attractive and engaging, helping to lure readers in. For new builds, there is an opportunity to design the overall architecture of the building to create an immersive reading space; The Treehouse Library in Singapore, is a wonderful example of this (see Case study 8.2 on page 161). In any library, regardless of budget or the size of the space, visual literacy can help to determine the layout of stock and shape the reader's journey, encouraging users to browse, explore, discover and interact with services in engaging ways. This can include the creation of areas for storytimes, for independent learning and study, or for perusing titles as part of collections. Well thought through visuals can give an easily identifiable brand and style that aids users in navigating the geography of the library space.

When considering the design of the physical space, think about the age and height of users, taking into account their sightlines and how they will encounter the library. Pay attention to light sources, where are the points where natural light falls and what artificial lighting is needed? Is there a way to incorporate colour or effects to create drama, impact or interest for particular displays? Are there ways of altering lighting to emphasise event space or to draw the eye to promotional spaces helping to focus attention and draw the gaze? Can lighting contribute to the atmosphere that makes the space immersive?

Choice of colour palettes can also have a profound impact upon the environment. Do you want the space to stimulate and engage, or to provide an area of sanctuary? Colour choices may be informed by a particular image from a book or be associated with the library branding to build an overall aesthetic around this.

Vinyls

Using graphic vinyls in and around the library is a simple and effective way to add visual enhancements to your space and collections. As part of a Big Lottery funded refurbishment, Lancaster Library, a bustling city centre venue, worked with local literature development agency, Lancaster Litfest on a vinyl project. Through surveys and community consultation Lancaster harvested opinions and views on the library and different stock areas as well as photographs of library users. These were used to create high impact quotes in a variety of fonts and sizes and dramatic silhouettes of characters reading and using the library's resources. These were printed onto self-adhesive vinyls and stuck around the library to create a contemporary design style which reflects the community and its interests within the library.

Exciting Environments

The reading environment is an important one. There is great inspiration to be found in the exciting and unusual ways that spaces have been developed to create a reading environment. Here are a couple of examples that could be adapted for the library space. Laurence Anholt and his wife Catherine created a bookshop in Lyme Regis in Dorset, that was called 'Chimp and Zee's Bookshop by the Sea' (see Figure 8.2). It was built around an oak tree and created an imaginative and immersive environment for children to enter. Laurence discusses the shop:

Figure 8.2 *Laurence and Catherine Anholt's innovative 'Chimp and Zee's Bookshop by the Sea'* © Laurence Anholt 2019

Back in the 1990s, my wife Catherine and I decided to create a magical children's bookshop called CHIMP and ZEE, BOOKSHOP by the SEA. We both trained as artists, and I have always loved making things with my hands, so it was huge fun to create dozens of animatronic displays and colourful tableaus to delight our young visitors. We employed three members of staff and sold nothing but our own signed children's books. Upstairs was a storytelling area, and in the centre of the shop was a full-sized oak tree with roots at the foot of the stairs and handmade bronze leaves stretching into the roof space above. There was also a huge open book which kids could climb inside to read. The text on the cover said, 'A BOOK IS A DOOR.'

By bringing together and reflecting elements of the creativity and knowledge that exist within the realms of books, there are opportunities to create reading environments that engage and inspire. Seven Stories is the National Centre for Children's Books in the United Kingdom, founded by Elizabeth Hammill and Mary Briggs, both former children's librarians; it bases several of its tenets on similar principles to those of the library profession. The centre curates and designs exhibitions relating to themes or creators of children's books and there is learning that can be taken from this and applied to the library setting. Gillian Rennie (2019), senior curator, provided insight into how Seven Stories approach exhibitions:

> Curating and designing exhibitions brings together theory around visual literacy and an understanding of how children engage with materials. With the set of materials available Seven Stories established a consortium of museums and galleries to consult with over approaches to displays and exhibitions. Colin Grigg at the Tate (author of *Discovering Art: New Ways of Looking*, 1997, De Agnostini Editions) had a particular knowledge of the way children tend to have an understanding of pictures but how as we grow older it can be lost as value and cultural importance is attached more to the written word than pictures. He recognised this process of loss of confidence and value occurring in art gallery settings and ran a project around 'jumping into pictures' as a way of helping to consider thought around the meaning of lines and associations that colours can hold.

When curating an exhibition on picturebooks, Seven Stories were keen to incorporate Colin Grigg's experiences from art gallery settings into its exhibitions and to create graphics from the original material in their archival book collection. To ensure the integrity of original material was maintained, Seven Stories were careful to avoid imposing another visual aesthetic on top of the material being displayed. In setting up exhibitions, the centre tries to create areas devoted to the books, using graphics from the books themselves and see it as key to honouring the importance and integrity of the word and pictures that have been so carefully crafted to convey the message of the book.

Gillian explained that Seven Stories' main aim in curating picturebook exhibitions is to pull out and highlight what the author and illustrator are trying to do, while thinking about what would stimulate a child to become involved in the exhibition. There are lots of things they are trying to achieve around the exhibition space; having fun is the overriding aim, but feeling relaxed, and having the time and inclination to engage with, discover and respond to the work is extremely important, this might be through an interaction such as dressing up or doing a drawing. As the centre for children's books, Seven Stories wants people to read, interact, share stories and respond. When thinking in general terms or asking big questions it is often difficult to get results, but by using one book as a springboard for discussions, that is often where the best and richest responses happen. Gillian commented: 'when seeing original illustrations, children are amazed to see the vibrancy of the colours and lines and want to talk about it in a creative way. Those are the moments we want to replicate in the gallery.'

Seven Stories faces a huge battle with retention as people may decide the centre isn't for them or they have outgrown it, with some feeling that picturebooks aren't suitable for adult readers or they might hold negative attitudes towards graphic novels and comics. It is important to get across that reading pictures and understanding visual narrative does not require less skill than reading words, but that a very different skill set is used.

The first picturebook exhibition Seven Stories ran was based on Dick Bruna's *Miffy*, and it focused on the simplicity of line drawing. Dick Bruna's illustrations communicate a large amount in a very simple way; Bruna works to a very strict set of rules about how the characters look, which has contributed to making his work so iconic. During Anthony Browne's laureateship, Seven Stories held an exhibition based on his book, *Through the Magic Mirror*, which featured a tunnel and an apple bike – it was a prime example of deepening the relationship people have with visual literacy through interactive elements. The exhibition was split into themes or particular book titles with different elements built in to create an immersive experience that would make attendees really feel they have entered the world of the picturebook. By capturing and drawing out the same elements from the pictures in the books themselves into the exhibition, Seven Stories were able to leave hints, clues and signals about what is going on through what is happening around exhibition attendees. Some of the discussions sparked by the exhibitions could not have been done so easily without pictures, but, Gillian reflects that there is still a fight to be had against the perception that people using pictures to 'understand' is somehow remedial.

Gillian explained that relationships with publishers and authors are important for developing the exhibitions but how this works often depends on the nature of the exhibition. Sometimes this relationship grows out of interest that the publishers express, such as with the David McKee, *Elmer the Elephant* exhibition which was curated at the suggestion of publisher Andersen Press to recognise the anniversary of the *Elmer* books. When an exhibition focuses upon or features a particular book, publishers often feel that the chances of audiences going on to buy the book are high so they are quite supportive.

Building good relationships can be key to the success of these kinds of projects and using illustration for design and exhibitions means potential merchandising opportunities exist. The processes and thinking behind setting up their exhibitions can inspire libraries wishing to create a visual experience using existing illustration as part of their design and layout; helping them to find ways to make their spaces exciting and engaging.

Furniture

Carrying visual elements through into furnishings and decor can be an effective way to stimulate interest and appeal making libraries more welcoming, familiar and stimulating for children. Bespoke furnishings can be expensive but specialist library suppliers like Peters create a range of items which offer affordable options. These include beanbags in the style of Jim Field's characters, storytime rugs designed as Elmer the Elephant or featuring Nick Sharratt's work and Nibbles the Book Monster. They also supply a range of furnishings in bright, attractive colours and featuring natural images from woodlands. 'Made by Node', a company started by illustrator Chris Haughton, creates special Nepalese fairtrade rugs with several designs that are created by children's illustrators, www.madebynode.com.

Some libraries also make use of bespoke furniture to help carry through a story motif. These can be seen in the shelving of the picturebook library in Gangkeng Hakka town in China, see page 121 for further information about the town and its associated illustration awards.

Children's home-furnishing shops often also provide soft-toys or designed furniture that is themed to be child-friendly, using jungle or farmyard motifs. These can help to create more immersive environments while also being cost effective.

Murals

And then…He saw it! On the concrete wall. He gasped. For the concrete wall was covered with the brightest, most eye-scorching colours Bailey had ever seen. So many colours that no sign of concrete remained. Just… Emerald green! Ruby red! Sapphire blue! All whirling and wheeling together! A kaleidoscope of stars, circles, crescent moons, comets! Everything twirling and twisting! Churning and whirling! Swirling!

(Ridley, 1997)

Graffiti art is often overlooked but can be an incredibly powerful form of visual storytelling, using intense colour and incredible movement. Philip Ridley's *Scribbleboy* shone a light upon this and the rejuvenating impact that well created street art can have upon urban landscapes, bringing colour, movement and drama to drab concrete. Inspired by artwork he saw on the streets of the East End of London, *Scribbleboy* is a celebration of expression and the difference that art can make to our outlook not only on our immediate environment, but also on our lives. Philip Ridley (2019) is an author, photographer, film director, playwright and artist; here he discusses the graffiti art that inspired his novel:

There used to be a derelict block of flats around the corner to where I lived. I say 'block of flats', but it was actually a whole estate. The Powers That Be had moved everyone out of the place because they wanted to demolish it and build something swish and new. But, for whatever reason, they never got around to knocking it down. It was there for ages. A real eye sore. It used to depress everyone who saw it, including me. I had to pass it every day, and it always made me feel gloomy. And then, one day, I turned the corner expecting to see the gloomy grey of the abandoned estate when...I saw colour. Lots of colours. Neon bright and swirling. During the night, a graffiti artist (or artists) had covered one whole wall – a huge wall! – with the most brilliant kaleidoscope of shapes and colours. It was like looking at those images of distant galaxies the Hubble telescope sends back. Only this was better because...it was just around the corner from me. It put the biggest smile on my face. It made me feel better, not only about myself but about the whole street. It made everywhere and everyone feel happy. If magic can be defined as something that causes wonder, and transforms the way we see the world...then this graffiti was magic! Pure magic. And what's more...it was free. I could see it whenever I wanted. And it was the inspiration for my novel *Scribbleboy*. I never knew who painted this magical graffiti. But I owe them a huge thank you. And so does everyone who ever saw it.

As part of a promotion of Philip Ridley's work, Lancashire Libraries ran a competition for children to design their own graffiti art or tag. Special sheets featuring brick wall motifs were created for children to draw upon and collections of books on different artists were available to help inform their work.

In the Harris Library in Preston, a graffiti artist was commissioned to create a mural above a revitalised teenage section that was sited near the computers, the aim being that this would act as a hook for young people, visually denoting their space. Spray paints were used to create a modern, eye-catching visual sign and representing some of the ideas that young people themselves had hoped to see represented.

Working with artists

If you are looking to enhance the visual displays in your library or find creative ways to engage new audiences, working with artists and illustrators is a great way to draw more attention to your collections and inspire creativity in young people who visit the library.

As part of Wakefield's new Wakefield One library site, children's book illustrator Lynne Chapman worked with groups of children in Wakefield and Castleford. Lynne ran drawing workshops with children encouraging them to create their own characters in drawings. In Castleford, this was themed around tigers, inspired by the name of the Rugby League Team, Castleford Tigers and in Wakefield library, the children created their own characters. Children's images were scanned and digitally enhanced to increase colour contrast for printing. A composite picture was created by Lynne using the scanned images and also some of her own illustrations together with photographs of library books and trolleys to create an energetic and lively picture. This was printed onto wallpaper and used as a mural in the children's library, see Figure 8.3.

Figure 8.3 *Mural created for Wakefield One library by Lynne Chapman and local children.* Photograph © Jake Hope, 2019

When working with a limited budget, or looking to strengthen ties with your local community, inviting trainee illustrators or art students to collaborate on a visual project can be a good way to create opportunities for young people at the start of their careers while developing bespoke visuals for the library. As part of a library's outreach or partnership work, it is worth exploring the types of organisations in the locality and thinking through ways that mutual benefits might be achieved. Can librarians provide feedback on the work students are undertaking, or contribute seminars or learning sessions about popular styles? It might be that students can test their work on reading groups to gain feedback from target audiences. In return, students might be willing to contribute artwork for use in the library.

I worked with students from the University of Central Lancashire's (UCLAN) Illustration MA course when they were given the opportunity to create bookplates for the 'My Home Library Project'. This was a scheme which Children's Laureate Anne Fine set up in response to the fact that children's book ownership was declining. The idea was that a website would be created that made recommendations of where to find books and that well-known illustrators and cartoonists would design bookplates that could easily be downloaded, printed and stuck into books for individuals to curate a bespoke collection of titles for their own libraries.

By working with UCLAN, students had the opportunity for their artwork to be placed alongside existing illustrator's work – including individuals like Quentin Blake, Chris Riddell and Posy Simmonds – for the duration of the project. More information on the My Home Library project can be found at www.myhomelibrary.org.

Working with visual creatives can yield eye-catching and appealing results as can be evidenced in Case study 8.3, which looks at the Lancashire Reading Trail, where Lancashire County Council collaborated with illustrator Mei Matsuoka. Whether you are working with an established artist or students, it is important that you set a clear brief to outline the aims of the project, expectations of the work that is involved, timescale and deadlines and the opportunity it presents to the artist. By setting a clear brief at the beginning of a project, all partners are on the same page at the outset. See some top tips below for creating a brief.

Creating an artist brief

1. What is the project? Be clear about what the project entails and its aims.
2. Who are the audience? It is important to identify who the target audience are and whether there are any special considerations for the artist to take into account. Where time can be factored into the project, some form of consultation with children and young people can really help to ensure finished materials are well targeted. Think about potential groups that might be useful to consult with.
3. What artwork is needed? Try to ensure that you are clear about the deliverables required, being clear on any limitations in terms of size and scale, colour reproduction etc. Try to find a balance between the project constraints and allowing the artists creative freedom.

4. What are the stages required to create the artwork? It is likely this will be determined, in part, by the timescale allotted for the project as a whole. If the artwork is being submitted via a competition, it is important to allow sufficient time for all participants to create their work and for this to be judged (with constructive feedback given). Where an individual is engaged to create work, ensure there is time for roughs to be created and approved. This is an important stage to ensure adherence to the brief and needs of the project. Allowing time for roughs ensures that amendments can be made. If you have conducted any audience consultation, roughs could be shown to this group for feedback.
5. What are the timescales for completion of the artwork? Be clear from the outset of all deadlines, including factoring in time for roughs to be approved and amendments made. If there will be a subsequent print element to the project, it is important to factor in time for this to happen.
6. What kind of opportunities does this offer for the artists? Exposure may be a key opportunity for the artist and if the project has practical application this could be beneficial to the artist in developing their portfolio. Project leads can offer testimonials and/or act as referees. You should also consider if there will be any financial remuneration offered, or, if not if there is any in-kind support that the library service is able to offer (e.g. opportunities for exhibition space, access to charged services, use of resources).

Case studies

Having explored opportunities to build the reading offer with visual literacy across stock, space and services, the next section of the book explores a number of case studies that provide a useful foundation for staff who are interested in running activities or projects.

Case study 8.1   The Lakes International Comic Art Festival

The Lakes International Comic Art Festival is a strong example of how visual images can be used to create a culture of reading across a whole community. The festival runs for a weekend and sees participants coming from across the globe.

While individual events can cause a great spike of interest in reading and engaging with visual literacy, themed festivals can reach critical mass and generate a momentum unlike any other. The Lakes International Comics Festival is an interesting example. The festival was developed to follow a European model, where events and activities take place over the whole community. A good example of this is Angoulême in France, where the festival takes over the town with the idea being that events with creators provide a professional backbone, but that there are also numerous opportunities for direct and active participation with street art, shop window displays and competitions and activities occurring in schools and colleges. The festival seeks to immerse people into the world of comics and graphic novels.

A range of different skill sets were brought together in establishing the festival, including the academic, libraries and education sector alongside creators. This gave the festival a strong reach and a range of approaches that could be demonstrated in funding bids. The academic wing involves Kendal College of Art and Lancaster University who have a visiting comics professor. The academic strand is branded as the 'thought bubble' and occurs a day before the main festival, but is nonetheless open to the general public. One of the aims of the festival was to try to reach an audience beyond 'comic aficionados' and to grow the market.

Doctor Mel Gibson, based at the University of Northumbria, is involved with handling activities and talks in the local library as well as with helping to provide and curate graphic artists. Mel has run various workshops with artists including multi award-winning illustrator Satoshi Kitamura and popular comic authors, the Etherington Brothers. Additionally, Mel has run sessions with adults to introduce graphic novels and information based sessions, which mix slideshows with question and answer discussions, providing a bridge into greater scholarly understanding of comics.

The team are highly experienced in delivering festivals. Their programming brings together street art, music and comics. Year on year the festival has grown in terms of reach and in its ability to attract international participants and acclaim. It has a different feel to many comic festivals and is funded by the Arts Council rather than having grown solely out of fandom.

Case study 8.2   My Treehouse Library, Singapore

From the Yggdrasil tree of Nordic legend, to Enid Blyton's *Magic Faraway Tree* or Andy Griffiths and Terry Denton's brilliantly inventive *13-Storey Treehouse* series, a parallel between knowledge, imagination and trees has long existed. This has formed the base for an exciting visual experiment and indeed experience in Singapore's Central Library. Aimed at children aged between 0 and 12, the library is an immersive visual environment that encourages discovery, learning, creativity and play. Carrying environment messages through its layout and visuals, the library has been designed around the concept of a woodland area, but is also home to a collection of 45,000 print books.

Figure 8.4 *A collection of photographs of the My Treehouse Library in Singapore* © Central Public Library Singapore, 2019

The centrepiece of the library is a huge tree whose trunk has been constructed from recyclable materials including aluminium, steel and wood. This branches into an impressive canopy whose individual leaves are formed of thousands of recycled plastic bottles collected from the public. Sustainable carpeting, gives the appearance of a forest floor.

This visual motif extends into the collection itself which is housed upon tree themed shelving units built from the libraries former units and refurbished using sustainable materials. The collection draws influence from the theme with around 30% of the stock focusing on topics pertaining to the environment – flora, fauna, habits, conservation and climate change – fiction too draws influence from the library layout with fairytales, folk-lore and fantasy being well represented.

Technology has also been embedded into this visual motif with a knowledge tree: an interactive wall that allows children to engage with and learn about the environment and conservation. There are also e-reading terminals tucked away in leafy nooks.

Reading areas are available and there is comfortable seating in the form of ladybirds, as well as a myriad of woodland and fairytale forest inspired décor to discover. Offering the services of a traditional library with an innovative and carefully designed visual layout that carries key environmental messages makes this a truly stand out library. With unique visuals that are carefully woven through the user experience, it has received excellent feedback such as the below taken from Tripadvisor reviews (2019):

> The children's library at the basement is definitely one of the prettiest and most awesome, with a treehouse made of upcycled materials set up for the little readers, and a plethora of books to choose from, and in so many languages too, and literally books for all ages (from age zero!). Plenty of space and the clean carpets meant the little ones can enjoy reading at any corner of this children's library.

Case study 8.3   Lancashire Reading Trail

The Lancashire Reading Trail is an example of a project that used illustration and design to help make services attractive to child users and to encourage wider reading. The scheme was created to encourage children to read 50 books, to stimulate knowledge about the library and to encourage wider reading as well as supporting children to learn more about the cultural offer available in Lancashire.

The project began by identifying an appropriate illustrator who would be commissioned to draw up a range of characters that would form the base for the visual assets for the scheme. The illustrator was required to take part in consultation with children across Lancashire to inform their designs. Mei Matsuoka – who had visited the authority as part of its children's book festival and other launches and so was familiar with the area and staff – was selected as the illustrator.

Mei was briefed about the project which would result in a new reading scheme for which it was anticipated she would illustrate no more than 12 characters using mixed media. Arrangements were made for Mei to meet and consult with groups of children from across the county to get a feeling for their tastes, likes, dislikes and interests in order to cumulate this knowledge and use it to help inform the project. Children were consulted from bookclubs, Brownie and Cub groups and local schools. During the consultative sessions, children had the opportunity to draw characters, talk about heroes and villains in some of the stories they enjoy and discuss their reading tastes and interests.

This information was then used as the basis to create twelve different re-invented fairytale characters including the Reading Dragon, the Cotton Wool Sheep and the Reading Fairies. Each was used to create collector cards which featured library-based tasks and information about the venue they were sited in. Bookmarks, shelf-wobblers, posters and maps were also created including die-cut standees.

Figure 8.5 *Materials created for Lancashire County Council's Lancashire Reading Trail illustrated by Mei Matsuoka.* Materials © Lancashire County Council; photos © Jake Hope, 2019

On starting the challenge, each child is given a special collector's map. For each book which they read, they receive a foot-print sticker which gets added to the map enabling them to progress further and further on the trail. At key progress points they receive a collector's card featuring one of the illustrated characters for the scheme and on completing ten books they receive a bronze certificate and on 25, a silver certificate. The cards all feature a library-based task, suggestions for a genre to try or an area of the library to explore. The card also features information about one of Lancashire's cultural venues which they are encouraged to visit. When they complete the map they will have collected all of the character cards, and receive a gold certificate.

As a digital element for the scheme, children have the opportunity to write and submit reviews which are then added to the library catalogue for the books children had selected to read. Thousands of children have participated and completed the award since it began in 2010. Once the challenge is completed, children are invited to a special ceremony where they receive a gold certificate; the cremonies have been held regularly and are a much anticipated feature in many libraries around the county, generating local media attention.

Case study 8.4   Wild in Art – Book Art Trails

Wild in Art is an exciting organisation that has helped to put creativity on the map, building public art installations around localities and creating events that entertain, enrich and leave a lasting legacy. Wild in Art creates fibreglass art installations which are painted and create trails around towns. They worked on the Read Manchester initiative, which was developed out of an ongoing relationship with the National Literacy Trust that had begun with their 'Books about Town' project. The project had created book benches which were designed and illustrated by artists using iconic imagery from the world of children's books and reading. The benches themselves were developed in fibreglass and took inspiration from a metal model in the British Library. The plan for the scheme was to bring the power of sculpture, a physical object, and link this to other areas of life, in this instance books, reading and geography. The project was designed to create an installation, a bench that people could physically sit on, read books on and take photographs helping to reinforce visual messaging.

The National Literacy Trust have literacy hubs in many parts of the country. Following a successful owl trail – 'The Big Hoot' in Birmingham, an education project working with the children's hospital and producing a series of owls, including large-scale owls that were sponsored by businesses and smaller ones with schools – it was felt that a follow-up project with book benches and schools could be successful. 175 schools across the West Midlands had bought into the owl trail and received the 'Reading for Enjoyment' training package run by the National Literacy Trust so it was felt the same engagement could be generated for the book benches.

A meeting took place with the National Literacy Trust and two members of Manchester City Council who were employed by the library service and appointed to oversee delivery of the wider literacy hub initiative. The scheme was titled, 'Read Manchester' and a plan was developed to create a 'Read Manchester Book Trail' as a wider engagement initiative. 50 schools from Manchester were targeted to be involved and the intention was that each would work with children to design their own pictures for a book bench.

Wild in Art provided staffing resource, created a marketing campaign, which included a trail map, an online presence and collateral around the benches to contextualise these. Benches were subsidised and schools were able to opt for a large or a small book bench (the small benches being suitable for children's libraries and reading corners). The model was taken out to the marketplace through headteacher forums, contacting schools directly, emailing about the opportunity and sending hardcopy information via the post. Networking events were attended and local authority channels were also utilised. 56 schools signed up for the project including some from outside Manchester and in the Greater Manchester area – Thameside and Salford – showing the project had appeal and reach across traditional political and authority boundaries. Wood Street Mission, a children's charity helping children and families living on a low income, heard about the project and were keen to involve HMP Manchester. The city council was also keen to be involved and provide creative output to get men in the prison environment excited about reading, engaging the prisoners in positive activity and getting families involved.

Schools had the opportunity to buy the book bench by itself or upgrade to having 'Reading for Enjoyment' National Literacy Trust training. 26 individuals from 19 schools signed up to this training. This was held at Z Arts in Manchester in two parts: an initial full day followed by a subsequent twilight session to share experiences and learning. Benches were delivered in the second week in January and all schools were invited to a briefing session where they were provided with information about the sculptures and the materials they could use on these as well as receiving a resource pack which detailed dos and don'ts about how to create and produce their book bench designs. Schools took different approaches to their designs; some engaged the whole school in designing the book bench, some worked with children, parents or teachers and some engaged the children with high learning potential, pupil premium or those with better artistic skills. The resource pack included cross-curricular learning ideas and reading lessons, as well as books and themes to spark imagination. Schools had a deadline to complete their bench designs. While schools were engaged in creating the designs, Wild in Art located host venues where they could be displayed. Libraries were integral to this and the benches were also used as a means for driving people into other cultural hubs including museums, art galleries and other cultural venues. Shopping centres were used as they had high footfall and were very accessible. Venues were gifted the installations, but were tasked with coming up with a programme of events and activities to promote reading for pleasure literacy. This included creative writing workshops, storytelling sessions, book signings, dressing up days and *Alice in Wonderland* themed events at the Lowry theatre. All of the events were specifically designed and targeted for different age groups.

The second phase of the project, where people were invited to tour the benches, was launched at the Children's BBC summer social which was themed around literacy and reading. 18 venues hosted the 56 sculptures. Sculptures were installed in early July so teachers still had opportunity to take children there before the summer holidays. Illustrated trails and activity maps listed all the venues and activities so that people could tick them off as they visited them over the summer holidays. All schools were sent copies of the trail map (45,000 produced in total).

A stakeholder launch event was held where schools could bring up to five learners and two teachers. This was held at Stoller Hall near Cheethams library, the oldest public library in the United Kingdom. Sculptures were collected in mid-September where they were returned to schools for legacy. Feedback showed that the schools that took part recognised the value in aligning the visual arts with the literacy process and that this drove people that would not ordinarily have visited the cultural venues towards them. Activities were well attended and the online presence and social media push aided awareness.

James Ramsbotham CBE (n.d.), Chief Executive North East England Chamber of Commerce, highly advocated for the scheme and encouraged the community to take part:

> Wild in Art events genuinely touch people's hearts. There are very few things involving the business community which reach out to people of every generation with such passion. Brand building is all about feelings and emotions and endears businesses to people and communities in a totally unique manner. Employees, customers, suppliers and their families, neighbours and the wider community will all become engaged. Go for it and show another side to you and your business.

Wild in Art has recognised the power, immediacy and potency of children's illustrations for installations in their own right. They have built several of their projects around children's books and comics. These have included the *Elmer the Elephant* parades, featuring David McKee's patchwork elephant, *The Snowdog* installations and *Oor Wullie* up in Edinburgh.

Figure 8.6 *Wild in Art book bench featuring the 2018 Carnegie Medal winning novel, Where the World Ends by Geraldine McCaughrean, published by Usborne Books*

Case study 8.5   Secret Slough Photography Project

Secret Slough took place over three days during the summer holidays. Led by Antonia Gray, the target audience was teenagers who went out into Slough and photographed images of their environment, the places that mattered to them or which they felt defined the area for them. The pictures were digitally manipulated, printed and used to create an exhibition in both digital and physical forms as well as being used to create black and white posters.

   The project aimed to engage teenagers in an activity that they would enjoy and which would provide them with skills that could be applied across a range of situations. It sought to positively affirm a sense of place and pride among community, to contribute towards ideas of digital citizenship through use of digital cameras and photographic manipulation software as well as use of PowerPoint to create digital exhibition. The photographs were archived at Slough History Online to create a permanent legacy from the project. The project had to be gender neutral and provide transferable skills.

The photographic project was felt to broach both the creative arts and build aptitudes around technology. A local photographer was engaged to deliver sessions and ensure sharing of knowledge. The team at Slough worked in collaboration with Creative Partnerships, an organisation built around creating partnerships that positively impact on the learning of young people. The project was timed to tie in with the Summer Reading Challenge run by The Reading Agency that was themed around 'The Reading Mission.'

The project was jointly funded by Creative Partnerships, Slough Estates and Masterfoods and was marketed to the local press through posters and on the library website. Although advertised for 12 to 16 year olds, ultimately all participants were 12 to 14.

Day One of the project saw participants learning key principles of photography. They were introduced to ways of seeing creatively and a range of photographic techniques. Participants worked in groups to discuss how images did or did not work. Young people were issued with digital cameras after an induction and practiced with these in the library before going out in supervised groups to take photographs around the town. The brief was that they should capture details that would normally go unseen or unnoticed but that they felt offered a unique insight into the town.

Day Two saw the young people using Adobe Photoshop as a tool to edit and manipulate the images they had taken. Each participant was encouraged to choose two colour photographs which would be mounted, creating one black and white photo for a poster and then creating a PowerPoint exhibition in order that as many images as possible were used.

Day Three was spent finalising the PowerPoint presentation, writing captions to accompany the pictures and mounting the colour photographs which had been processed overnight. Once this was complete, library staff finalised the presentations, oversaw printing of posters and physically managed and hung the exhibition.

The exhibition was opened by the town's mayor and participants' posters were displayed on the walls while colour photographs were displayed and mounted on exhibition boards. The project gave a sense of ownership to the town – linked with digital citizenship – and provided extracurricular learning and skills acquisition for young people during the summer months. The project was featured in CILIP's *Update* magazine.

A participant in the project commented that they had found it 'a useful course for life...different, excellent, funky, fascinating, fun.'

Case study 8.6   A Sense of Place

The Sense of Place project was run by the library service in Lancashire in conjunction with the virtual schools team who have responsibility for children that are looked after in residential care. It formed an extension for a larger project, 'NE14 Reading' which recognised the fact that young people in residential care often move between settings numerous times creating difficulties in settling and in having consistent access to formal education. 'NE14 Reading' recognised the role of literacy as the access point for learning. It sought to provide collections of books aimed at reading for pleasure in residential care homes alongside opportunities for kinaesthetic learning activities. A Sense of Place was one such project and aimed to create a curated collection of poetry that would be written and performed by young people before being recorded onto CDs which would be professionally printed and placed into display cases. These would then be used to help welcome young people arriving in residential care, providing access to a range of young people's thoughts, opinions and experiences through poetry.

As part of the project, the young participants were invited to explore different urban and graffiti artists including individuals like Banksy, J Besset, Goddog and Keith Haring. The participants were encouraged to draw accompanying illustrations in the style of graffiti artists and these were given to a young trainee in design at a local youth group. He assembled these into a Keith Haring style visual motif which became the cover image for the CD box and part of the printed design on the CD itself giving distinct visual branding that was informed and created by young people.

Conclusion

Books can be without borders, pictures can show us routes into the past, present and also into possible futures. Through looking at the history of visual literacy, many of the aspects and considerations involved in its creation and use, it is hoped that readers will have an increased understanding of the role it is able to play in our daily lives. The guidance and case studies that the book ends with will hopefully stimulate thinking and applied use, helping to increase confidence and awareness among practitioners as to the impact that visual literacy is able to play in young people's reading and creativity.

Vivian French (2019), author and co-founder of the Picture Hooks initiative, which aims to provide illustrators with mentors and development opportunities, is well-versed in using visuals as a means for stimulating children's creativity. She discusses her approach:

> I regularly run writing/illustration workshops for children, often with an illustrator, and in my experience prioritising the visual aspect works wonderfully well. Hopefully it feels more like participatory play than serious literary application.
>
> Children respond with such enthusiasm to pictures; I find that they all too often describe 'writing' as boring and formulaic. Illustrations are enticing, not threatening – a wonderful springboard to encourage a class to actually WANT to use their imagination and create a story.
>
> Very briefly, I work like this:
>
> I ask for a feeling, and we discuss who has the feeling... and why... and we draw the character. Then, I ask, if this is the beginning of the story, how does the character feel at the end? And we draw that. What's the difference? What has changed? WHY has it changed?
>
> This leads to what I call the story map, where we link the beginning and end together – and at every stage I ask the children for their ideas. It's hugely important to state that no idea is ever a bad idea – if it's not

appropriate for the story, put it in a 'brilliant ideas' box for use another time, and collect more suggestions before choosing the best.
Encouragement and enthusiasm are so essential... story writing should be FUN!

Visual literacy can invigorate and inspire so many areas of reading and of library provision, helping to make settings immersive, meanings immediate and services enticing. It offers creative opportunities to re-think the ways that we present books and some of the activities that can be built around them. Working across services, stock and space allows a holistic approach to visual reading development.

Olivia Lomenech Gill, print-maker, artist and illustrator, frequently talks about seeing the extraordinary in the ordinary. It feels apt to close the book with her observation which highlights how learning to really see can be an ongoing process and one which alters our perception and understanding:

Sit long enough to look at an object and really study it and you begin a journey of discovery.

Afterword

Nick Sharratt

I've been a children's book illustrator for more than 30 years now, producing imagery practically every day, and I'm still finding out about my craft and learning new things as regards the wider world of visual literacy. I've certainly made fresh discoveries with this book (and am thrilled to have added 'plewds' and 'squeans' to my vocabulary!).

Working alone in my studio, I've always felt that I create instinctively, in that I never quite know what it is that I'm after until I've found it, although it's generally pretty clear to me when something isn't going the right way. So it's been an affirmative experience to see, discussed and made real in the preceding chapters, the myriad factors that are involved, whether consciously or subconsciously, in the image-making process. It's been revelatory too, to learn how fellow illustrators make decisions about things like technique, composition and colour, and to read about what influenced them in their formative years.

I don't have children and when I create my books I rely to a large degree on going back to my own childhood and remembering what engaged me as boy – the things I found interesting, appealing and funny. I've a good memory for those early years, and I can recall with particular vividness certain books I absorbed, whether bought for me or borrowed from the library. To be more precise, I remember pictures in those books, images that are seared forever in my brain and affect me to this day.

Those images fall into two distinct categories. There were the painterly illustrations used in some of my picture books, and synonymous with the Ladybird 'readers' that my generation grew up with. Only, to my young mind (and everyone of my generation I've ever discussed it with) those images weren't painted – they were real. We were all able to step right into the pages and join Peter and Jane, or the characters from the 'Well-loved Tales' series (my own favourites were *The Elves and the Shoemaker* and *The Princess and the Pea*) in their sensory worlds, feeling the sunshine or rain

Figure A.1 *Library card and joining leaflet for Lancashire County Council's library service featuring Nick Sharratt's popular* Shark in the Park *imagery*

on our faces, the grass, sand or snow beneath our feet, entering inside the buildings, sitting on the furniture, touching the fabrics, tasting the food. I relished the fabrics and the food in particular. I would gaze at the shoemaker's tiny scraps of coloured leather and feel the warm softness on my fingers. I would spot a little cake in a 'Peter and Jane' book, topped with white icing and a red cherry, and my tastebuds would tingle alarmingly (no written description of food has ever caused triggered the same reaction). Similarly, if I start thinking about Pierre Leroy's beautifully atmospheric and rather unsettling images in *The Story of Man* I get goose pimples all over my arms.

In my head I remember and feel the intensity of my responses to these pictures when I encountered them more than 50 years ago. I have a few of the books in front of me at the moment and the thing is, I still get great pleasure from the brilliant artwork, but as an adult something has faded: the enviable, truly magical gift children have to make an illustration on a page become completely and utterly alive. The power of a child's imagination! It's recalling how it felt to look at these books through young eyes that is so significant to me now.

There was another style of picture book that entranced me as a boy. With these books I could still lose myself in the illustrations, but because of the stylised nature of the drawing and being able to recognise the materials used, I was much more conscious of the mark making and I was fascinated by it. These pictures made me want to draw. Their impact continues to this day. Every time flowers are called for in my illustrations my head fills with the spectacle of Michael Foreman's gorgeous meadow of red, purple and blue flowers in *The General*. Whenever I'm rendering an area of grass, I recall the pleasure gained from Anita Lobel's fields in *The Little Wooden Farmer*, and how I loved that she'd taken the trouble to draw every single tiny blade. I give lots of my characters big round rosy cheeks, connecting directly with my enjoyment of Alison Prince's cast of red cheeked characters in her 'Joe' stories. I looked at these books again and again and absorbed so much from the pictures they helped determine my own style of drawing in the years to come.

Growing up in the late sixties and early seventies, I was attracted too, to the pop-art style of the illustrations I saw in my mum's magazines, on children's TV, on food packaging and on things like the groovily designed sleeves for the children's records that occasionally came my way. The dazzling, exuberant colours and the cartoon-like graphics combined to create a sense of fun that I found irresistible. Again I wanted to make pictures like that.

I'm not from an artistic background, but I will be forever grateful to my parents for taking seriously, right from the start, something they could sense was important to me. I was never short of drawing paper, crayons, poster paint or – my preferred medium – felt tipped pens. (Once I was old enough to have a paper round, all my wages would go on felt-tipped pens.) Every birthday or Christmas I would be given some new kind of art material that I'd experiment with, for a while, before returning to my beloved felt tips.

I was encouraged at school too. My self-confidence and belief in my artistic skills were boosted enormously when I took in a picture that I'd drawn at home to show my teacher, and she put it on display in the school hall for a whole term. That incident just about much sealed my fate – from then on I was determined I was going to make my living as an artist.

But although the praise received for my art at primary and secondary school (from both teachers and fellow pupils) was hugely important, I have next to no recollection of actually being taught anything in art lessons – as I remember it, we were just given a subject to explore and left to get on with it. I had enough enthusiasm and self-discipline to get something out of those afternoons in the art room, but others in the class could have benefitted so much from a bit of practical guidance and instruction. These days I do what I can to encourage art and the creative thinking associated with it, with all its pleasures and benefits. For the past couple of years I've held scores of 'Drawalong' events in theatres and arts centres, where children and adults come along armed with paper and pencils and spend an hour or so drawing with me. I always start by saying there are no actual rules here other than that drawing should be fun, then I show, step by step, how I might go about sketching a character or an animal, and the audience follows my suggestions. For many present (the events are for four years old and up) it will be the first time they have drawn something with such deliberation, and the resulting images have been truly amazing.

I've met thousands of children over the decades, at drawalongs, and also in schools and libraries in every part of the country. I'm always hoping to inspire but I've constantly been inspired too. Many's the time, after a particularly brilliant day of interaction, I've come away with the glowing seed of an idea which has then evolved into an actual book. Thank you to all the teachers and librarians who were instrumental in making days like that happen.

Returning to the books of my youth, another of my favourite Ladybirds was the gloriously illustrated *The Story of Houses and Homes*. The final picture is of a 'modern' 1960s house, and through the plate glass window, a stylish red armchair can be glimpsed, angled for taking in the view. I spent a lot of time transporting myself into that living room and swivelling contentedly in that chair. When I came to illustrate what is probably my most popular picture book, *You Choose*, naturally I included the chair on the 'Furniture' page. And around the same time I finally purchased for myself a red chair identical to the one in the picture that had obsessed me since I was seven.

Glossary

Acrylics – acrylics are water-based paints. This means they are able to be cleaned and thinned with water. They can give the appearance of oil paints but are often more practical to use as they are faster and easier to clean up. As acrylic paints are water soluble, they can also be thinned to give the appearance of watercolours.

Background – a compositional term for objects or subjects found in the rear portion of an image.

Binding – a production technique which determines how pages are held together to form the book, this is commonly sewn or glued (also known as perfect binding).

Bleeds – a term to describe when an image reaches the extremity of the page, the name comes from the fact that the ink literally bleeds off the page, it can create visual intensity and immersion and can also suggest the scene extends beyond the audience's field of vision.

Blocking in – an early process in painting where the initial colours and shapes are added to a canvas, this is commonplace for oil paintings and helps outline the overall composition and use of colour.

Captions – common in graphic novels, captions are used to carry narration or voice over, elements that are necessary to the story progression but are not direct speech.

Charcoal – a dry art material that is traditionally made using peeled twigs which are heated in the absence of oxygen. Charcoal allows free sketching and is well suited to loose line images. It can be smudged easily with the fingers unless held in place with a fixative. This can be used to create effects of blurring.

Close up – a close up or macro is an image that draws the viewer's attention to the object of focus in a heightened level of detail.

Colour – the result of wavelengths of light that are visible to the eye. The associations that colours hold have historical and cultural connotations that affect mood and understanding.

Composition – this can apply either to individual illustrations or to the design of a page and refers to how elements are arranged together to create the overall structure or image.

Counterpoint – the interpretative or imaginative space that exists between words and pictures in illustrated text. This can empower early visual readers who listen to the words and see the differences shown in the pictures.

Cross cutting – when a sequence in a narrative crosses over with that of another.

Cross-hatching – a drawing technique for creating shading and form, similar to hatching but here lines intersect with one another often resulting in a denser appearance.

Debossing – a process for making areas on a page appear concave. This can be used to create tactile elements.

Die-cut – a technique for cutting shapes or holes into books. The die is a blade formed into a particular shape or pattern used to cut holes into paper or board.

Drybrush – a technique where a small amount of paint is used on a relatively dry brush. This is usually applied to a coating layer of paint that has already dried and is useful as a finishing process to provide highlights, dimension and additional texture.

Emanata – lines around a characters head indicating a feeling of surprise.

Embossing – a process for making areas on a page stand out in relief, this can be used to create tactile elements.

Establishing shot – an image which opens a work or new scene.

Extent – the number of pages which comprise a publication, in picturebooks this is commonly 32.

Eye level – use of perspective which is at eye level and which therefore can create an intimacy or union between focal characters and the reader.

Fade – a technique where an image is blurred and fades out to suggest either change of focus or the end of a particular sequence. Fading can also be used to create soft edges for a particular image.

Flashback – use of images that carry the reader back from the main narrative to a previous point in time.

Foil blocking – a process whereby metallic film is added to the surface of paper. These can be in a variety of shades or colours and can add vibrancy to book jackets.

Foreground – a compositional term for objects or subjects found in the front portion of an image.

Frame – a frame is an individual illustration that is boxed commonly by a border or by the edges of the art itself (these may be hard, where they are well defined, or soft, where they fade out).

Graphic weight – this is use of light and dark toned images or patterning to draw the eye to particular areas that might carry significance in the overall picture.

Grawlix – the use of font symbols in place of expletives @~!"

Gutter – the area on a double page spread where the pages converge during binding, this can be used compositionally to separate areas, or it may be that a gutter margin is employed to avoid elements being 'lost' during the production process.

Hatching – a drawing technique used for the creation of shading and form using parallel lines usually travelling the same direction.

High angle – perspective which provides a higher angle giving the reader the experience of looking down on a particular scene or image.

Hue – the specific artistic term for different types of colour.

Impasto – the application of thick layers of paint using a palette knife to achieve a painterly heavily textured effect.

Impressionism – an artistic style reflecting everyday life but capturing this with spontaneity. Artwork tends to be influenced by effects of light and darkness at particular moments.

Ink – the pen and ink tradition has a long pedigree in illustration. Different types of pen can result in varying line style and quality, achieved through the width of the nib and by the rate of ink flow. Types of pen include fountain pens, graphic pens, reed pens, brush pens, ball point pens and even quills. Inks can come in cartridges, as part of pens themselves or in bottles of varying shades. Quentin Blake created a series of ornithological illustrations using quills made from feathers of each of the species he drew. Pen and ink illustrations have a long history of being used for illustrating books including George Cruikshank, caricaturist and illustrator for Charles Dickens and Edward Ardizzone the inaugural winner of the CILIP Kate Greenaway Medal.

Intaglio printmaking – is usually carried out upon metal plates (often made of copper – copper-plate fonts derive their name from this process – zinc or steel). Grooves are engraved into the plate using sharp implements or through the corrosive action of a strong acid solution.

Ink is worked into the plate and the surface wiped clean before pressure is exerted by a press resulting in dampened paper taking the ink.

Lamination – a design technique which sees the application of a thin layer of plastic to a page, this can make colours appear more vibrant and can also make books and print more durable.

Lithographic printing – this uses wet ink and rollers. It tends to produce higher quality printing than digital print, but requires significant set-up.

Low angle – perspective which provides a lower angle giving the reader the experience of looking up on a particular scene or circumstance.

Midground – a compositional term for subjects or objects placed in the middle of an image. Often this is the area that the eye is drawn to first.

Mixed media – composite images constructed from a range of different artistic media.

Monochrome – a method of reproduction that uses only one colour of ink and which utilises different shades to give density and form. This is commonly black and white.

Motif – a recurring visual which gives a weight of significance to a particular theme or subject.

Movement lines – lines on an object or character which indicate force, momentum and often direction of travel.

Naturalism – an artistic style where objects are depicted realistically as seen and experienced in the everyday world.

Oil paints – as the name suggests, oil paint is made by mixing pigments of colour together with an oil medium. The oil used in paint is commonly linseed oil, but can include poppy seed, walnut and safflower oils. Oil paints tend to have a greater ratio of pigment in them which allows for the production of more vivid and saturated colours. Oil paints take a long time to dry which makes them easy to mix. Once dried, oil paints can endure for many hundreds of years; an example of this is the recently discovered paintings in Bamiyan, Afghanistan, these date back to approximately 650 AD and are significant for pre-dating the previously earliest known use of oil paintings. Oil paints are, however, an expensive option and this combined with the intensity of their colour pigmentation mean they lend a lavish and painterly aesthetic to works.

Page turns – a key moment of pace, plot and progression when suspense or anticipation is built up before the reader turns the page to find out what happens next.

Pan – through use of panels, graphic novels are often able to shift the focus across a particular vista or landscape.

Panels – a panel is when a series of framed illustrations are held in sequence, they commonly denote a relationship which shows the passage of time or of movement through landscape.

Panorama – images which show a broad view of a particular scene. This can also be achieved through use of a length of tiered panels that cumulatively show a single view.

Papercut – images composed using cut pieces of paper.

Pastels – pastels are produced from powdered pigments, meaning they offer saturated colour. Pastels can be hard, soft or oil. They can also come in pencils. Pastels can be easily blended using fingers, meaning there can be direct input from the creator.

Pencils – these can be coloured or monochrome using varying degrees of hard and soft graphite. Pencils are commonly used for sketching and often illustrators will use these to create storyboards and roughs. Colours can easily be blended together to create a vast number of shades, tints and hues.

Perspective – the focal point from which the audience sees what is being depicted, this can also be termed point of view. The term can also be used to refer to the methods for giving an image the appearance of three-dimensionality.

Photorealism – an artistic style whereby the artist seeks to create images that appear photographic.

Plewds – teardrop shaped beads of sweat shown disseminating from a character and used to show anxiety or stress.

Pointillism – an artistic style growing out of theories of sight, it involves the application of isolated dots or points to cumulatively form an image when viewed from a distance.

Pop Art – art which draws focus from popular culture and everyday imagery.

Realism – an artistic style where the common man and everyday pursuits are depicted.

Recto – the formal term, often used in production, to identify a page on the right hand side of a publication.

Relief printmaking – this is where the artist has cut away areas not requiring inking during the printing process, leaving raised portions which make contact with the print-material. This can be done as woodcut, where a drawing is made onto wood where negative areas are cut away, or on linocut which can be cut more easily, but is long-lasting and hard-wearing.

Romanticism – an artistic style where images are influenced by human mood and emotions.

Saturation – the level of intensity of a colour, mixing hues with white lowers the saturation and creates a tint of the original hue.

Screen printing – using a stencil through which paint is forced. Every colour printed requires a different screen to be used and so the image is composed through the layering of colours.

Scumbling – applying paint through the use of a cloth to lightly rub it on, this exposes elements of the colour beneath and achieves a mist like effect.

Sgraffito – a technical term for the removal of paint to expose the underpainting or surface. It is common in painting and also ceramics.

Shade – the dark values in a particular colour or hue.

Speech bubbles – also known as speech balloons, they relate direct speech as part of an image. The manner in which the bubble is produced can denote the force or volume of the speech. Dotted bubbles indicate a character is whispering whilst a spikey or emboldened outline suggests shouting.

Splash – a term commonly associated with graphic novels, this is a large illustration which fills most of, if not all, of a page and which breaks the flow of panels helping to create impact and establish mood, this makes them useful for opening new scenes.

Splattering – a technique used to create explosions of colour. It has perhaps been used most famously in the paintings of Jackson Pollock.

Sponging – applying paint using a sponge to create a richly textured application.

Squeans – stars, birds or the like that circle a character to indicate dizziness, intoxication or having suffered a blow to the head.

Stippling – a drawing or painting technique which uses dots to create shading and form, the higher the ratio of dots, the darker the appearance of shading. The effect is notable for its association with the Pointillism movement.

Surrealism – an artistic movement depicting ideas of the unconscious mind and the impact of these upon human thinking and dreams. The movement rejects logic in favour of free association.

Texturising – a technique in painting to add texture to an image, this might use the brush itself, or a range of other media and can help give the illusion of depth.

Thought cloud – these are used to show the thought or internal monologue of characters.

Tint – the light values in a particular colour or hue.

Tone – the level of light or dark in a composition, this can help to give the impression of light and of shadows in images.

Underpainting – a technique in painting where a layer of paint is applied to serve as a base. This aids in the creation of contrast.

Verso – the formal term, often used in production, to identify a page on the left hand side of a publication.

Visual explosions – sometimes called word bubbles, these are jagged shapes that often contain onomatopoeic sounds and are conventionally used in fight scenes such as 'Wham' or 'Kapow'.

Wash – the build-up of translucent layers of water colour – or thinned acrylic paints. Washes lack the appearance of brush strokes.

Watercolours – these are water-based paints which can be thinned with water. Watercolours are particularly notable for the translucent quality they can have. These are known as washes which lend themselves well to expansive vistas: skyscapes, landscapes and seascapes. Watercolours work well when combined with other media. The application of water upon existing painted areas allows for the layering of colour.

References

Arizpe, Evelyn and Styles, Morag, (2003) *Children Reading Pictures*, Routledge.

Bader, B. (1976) *American Picturebooks from Noah's Ark to The Beast Within*, Macmillan Publishing Company.

Barbe, Walter Burke, Swassing, Raymond H. and Milone, Michael N. (1979) *Teaching Through Modality Strengths: Concepts and practices*, Zaner-Bloser.

Briggs, Raymond (2015) Art Snobbery in *Notes from the Sofa*, Unbound.

Bronte, Charlotte, (1847) *Jane Eyre*, www.gutenberg.org/ebooks/1260.

Burmark, Lynell, (2008) Visual Literacy: What You Get is What you See, in Frey, Nancy and Fisher, Douglas, (2008) *Visual Literacy: Using Comic Books, Graphic Novels, Anime, Cartoons and More to Develop Comprehension and Thinking Skills*, Corwin Press.

Callow, J. (2005) Literacy and the Visual: Broadening our vision, *English Teaching: Practice and critique*, **4** (1), 6–19.

Carroll, Lewis, (1865) *Alice's Adventures in Wonderland*, www.gutenberg.org/ebooks/11

Child, Lauren (2018) Introduction, *Drawing Words*, British Council.

Commodari, E. (2017) Novice Readers: The Role of Focused, Selective, Distributed and Alternating Attention at the First Year of the Academic Curriculum, *i-Perception*, https://doi.org/10.1177/2041669517718557.

Day, Jess (2018) *Constructing bias – the wonky world of picture books*, Let Toys be Toys, http://lettoysbetoys.org.uk/constructing-bias-the-wonky-world-of-picture-books.

Debes, John (1969) cited in Harrison, Kirsten, *What is Visual Literacy?* (n.d.), Visual Literacy Today, https://visualliteracytoday.org/what-is-visual-literacy.

Eyre, Charlotte (2019a) Acevedo and Morris win Carnegie and Kate Greenaway Medals, *The Bookseller*, www.thebookseller.com/news/acevedo-and-morris-win-carnegie-and-kate-greenaway-medals-1022631.

Eyre, Charlotte (2019b) Lack of female and BAME characters in picture books angers industry figures, *The Bookseller*, www.thebookseller.com/news/white-and-male-characters-dominate-picture-book-bestsellers-1022391.

Fergusson, Donna (2019) 'Highly concerning': picture books bias worsens as female characters stay silent, *The Guardian*, www.theguardian.com/books/2019/jun/13/highly-concerning-picture-books-bias-worsens-as-female-characters-stay-silent.

Goldstein B. (2016) *Visual literacy in English Language teaching: Part of the Cambridge Papers in ELT series* [pdf], Cambridge University Press.

Gusti (2006) *Half of an Elephant*, Kane/Miller Book Publishers.

Hacking, Charlotte (2019) *The Power of Pictures: Summary of Findings from the Research on the CLPE Power of Pictures Project 2013–19*, Centre for Literacy in Primary Education.

Hendle, Mark, (2016) *New Children's Book Award: The Klaus Flugge Prize* [Press Release], retrieved from http://booksforkeeps.co.uk/childrens-books/news/new-children%E2%80%99s-book-award-the-klaus-flugge-prize.

Hodgson Burnett, Frances (1911) *The Secret Garden*, www.gutenberg.org/ebooks/113.

Hopwood, Mererid, (2019) *Geiriau Diflanedig: Finding Lost Words in Welsh*, www.cilip.org.uk/blogpost/1637344/330654/Geiriau-Diflanedig-Finding-Lost-Words-in-Welsh.

Kipling, Rudyard (1902) *Just So Stories for Little Children*, www.gutenberg.org/ebooks/2781.

Langrish, Katherine (2014) *The Colours in Fairytales*, Seven Miles of Steel Thistles, https://steelthistles.blogspot.com/2014/04/the-colours-in-fairytales.html.

Lindstrom, Robert (1994) *The Business Week Guide to Multimedia Presentations*, Osborne McGraw-Hill.

Lubecka, Anna (n.d.) Banana Bear Books, https://bananabearbooks.com/childrens-book-designer-london.

Mawle, Ali (n.d.) *How to 'read' a painting*, The National Gallery, www.nationalgallery.org.uk/learning/teachers-and-schools/teaching-english-and-drama/how-to-read-a-painting?viewPage=1.

McCabe, J., Fairchild, E., Grauerholz, L., Pescosolido, B. A., and Tope, D. (2011) Gender in Twentieth-Century Children's Books: Patterns of Disparity in Titles and Central Characters, *Gender & Society*, **25** (2), 197–226, https://doi.org/10.1177/0891243211398358.

Mix K. S., Sandhofer C. M., Moore J. A. and Russell C. (2012) Acquisition of the cardinal word principle: the role of input, *Early Childhood Research Quarterly*, **27** (2), 274–83, https://doi.org/10.1016/j.ecresq.2011.10.003.

Mould, Chris (2007) interviewed by Jake Hope, Three Illustrators, *ACHUKA*, www.achuka.co.uk/interviews/three_illustrators.php.

National Autistic Society (2002) *Do children with autism spectrum disorders have a special relationship with* Thomas the Tank Engine *and, if so, why?*, https://lemosandcrane.co.uk/resources.

Pickton, Lindsay and Chen, Christine (2019) *Use the Beano to Teach Key Reading Skills – Even to Reluctant Readers*, www.teachwire.net/news/use-the-beano-to-teach-key-reading-skills-even-to-reluctant-readers.

Ramsbotham, James (n.d.) *Q&A with James Ramsbotham CBE*, www.wildinart.co.uk/qa-with-james-ramsbotham-cbe.

Riddell, Chris (2007) interviewed by Jake Hope, Three Illustrators, *ACHUKA*, www.achuka.co.uk/interviews/three_illustrators.php.

Ridley, Philip (1997) *Scribbleboy*, Puffin Books.

Serafini, Frank (2014) *Reading the Visual: an introduction to teaching multimodal literacy*, Teachers College Press.

Serafini, Frank (2015) Paths to Interpretation: Developing Students' Interpretative Repertoires, *Language and Literacy*, **17** (3), 119–33, http://frankserafini.com/publications/serafini-paths-to-interpret.pdf.

Strick, Alex (n.d.) *Books and disability: advice for writers, illustrators and publishers*, BookTrust, www.booktrust.org.uk/books-and-reading/bookmark-disability-and-books/for-writers-illustrators-and-publishers.

Tan, Shaun (2004) *Picture Books: Who are They For?*, www.shauntan.net/essay1.html.

The Reading Agency (2018) *Summer Reading Challenge Family Survey 2018*, https://tra-resources.s3.amazonaws.com/uploads/entries/document/3213/FamilySurveyReport_2018_FINAL.pdf.

Tripadvisor user feedback (2019) *My Treehouse Library*, www.tripadvisor.co.uk/Attraction_Review-g294265-d1994786-Reviews-or10-National_Library_of_Singapore-Singapore.html.

Turvey, Kris (2017) interviewed by Meagan Meehan, Literacy Mystery: 'The Famous Five' books series and app game, *Blasting News*, https://us.blastingnews.com/gaming/2017/12/literary-mystery-the-famous-five-book-series-and-app-game-002218793.html.

Vellutino, F. R., Fletcher, J. M., Snowling, M. J. and Scanlon, D. M. (2004) Specific reading disabilities (dyslexia): what have we learned in the past four decades?, *Journal of Child Psychology and Psychiatry*, **45**, 40137−48.

Ward, Nick (2007) interviewed by Jake Hope, Three Illustrators, *ACHUKA*, www.achuka.co.uk/interviews/three_illustrators.php.

Weitzman, L. J., Eifler, D., Hokada, E. and Ross, C. (1976) Sex-Role Socialization in Picture Books for Preschool Children, *Sexism in Children's Books*, Writers and Readers Publishing Co-operative.

Werner, Abraham Gottlob and Syme, Patrick, (1814) *Werner's Nomenclature of Colours, with additions, arranged so as to render it highly useful to the arts and sciences*, James Ballantyne and Co.

Wiesner, David (2012) quoted in Marcus, Leonard, *Show me a story!: Why Picture Books Matter*, Candlewick.

Wisniewski, David (1997) *Acceptance Speech for Caldecott Medal*, www.ala.org/alsc/awardsgrants/bookmedia/caldecottmedal/ caldecotthonors/1997caldecott.

Wolf, Maryanne (2008) *Proust and the Squid*, Icon books.

Personal interviews

Agee, Jon (2019) 7 September

Anholt, Laurence (2019) 2 September

Antony, Steve (2019) 29 September

Baker, Jeannie (2019) 19 August

Beaton, Clare (2019) 29 August

Bently, Peter (2019) 9 September

Biesty, Stephen (2019) 22 September

Blackwood, Freya (2019) 10 September

Blake, Quentin (2019) 28 August

Blathwayt, Benedict (2019) 2 September

Brown, Ruth (2019) 2 September

Browne, Anthony (2019) 25 September

Brumwell, Alison (2019) 15 August

Cottrell-Boyce, Frank, (2019) 26 October

Court, Joy (2019) 5 September

Cowell, Cressida (2019) 14 August

Curry, Alice (2019) 13 September

Davies, Nicola (2019) 21 August

Eland, Eva (2019) 29 August

Fickling, David (2019) 13 September

Fine, Anne (2019) 12 July
Flugge, Klaus (2019) 6 September
Foy, Debbie (2019) 4 September
French, Vivian (2019) 10 January
Geras Adele (2019) 1 September
Gliori, Debi (2019) 9 September
Goodwin, Prue (2019) 23 August
Greet, Pauwelijn (2019) 26 September
Hanaor, Ziggy (2019) 2 September
Horacek, Petr (2019) 1 September
Hughes, Shirley (2019) 1 September
Jeffers, Oliver (2019) 15 October
Jenkins, Steve (2019) 9 December
Lomenech Gill, Olivia (2019) 19 October
Love, Jessica (2019) 28 July
MacFarlane, Robert (2019) 7 October
McIntyre, Sarah (2019) 7 August
McKay, Amy (2019) 18 June, 10 July, 29 September
Mistry, Poonam (2019) 9 September
Morris, Jackie (2019) 5 September, 19 September
Murphy, Adam, (2019) 29 September
National Library for Children and Young Adults, Republic of Korea
    (2019) 11 October
Onyefulu, Ifeoma (2019) 30 August
Packenham, Sarah (2019) 20 August
Pauwelijn, Greet (2019) 26 September
Powell, Isobel (2019) 15 August
Reed, Ben (2019) 20 September
Rennie, Gillian (2019) 26 September
Ridley, Philip (2019) 26 September
Roberts, David (2019) 30 September
Ross, Edward (2019) 26 August
Simmonds, Cate (2019) 3 June
Spiegelman, Art (2019) 16 August
Stirling, Mike (2019) 17 September
Styles, Morag (2019) 2 September
Talbot, Bryan (2019) 26 September
Thompson, Hermione (2019) 25 September

Wiesner, David (2019) 5 September
Willden-Lebrecht, Vicki (2019) 26 September
Wollard, Jessica (2019) 7 October
Yang, Gene Luen (2019) 9 September
Yu Rong (2019) 9 September
Zommer, Yuval (2019) 13 September

Index